ACADEMIC INTEGRITY AND STUDENT DEVELOPMENT:
☐ *Legal Issues and*
☐ *Policy Perspectives*

By William L. Kibler
Elizabeth M. Nuss
Brent G. Paterson
Gary Pavela

The Higher Education Administration Series
Edited by Donald D. Gehring and D. Parker Young
COLLEGE ADMINISTRATION PUBLICATIONS, INC.

© 1988 College Administration Publications, Inc.,
All rights reserved. Published 1988
Printed in the United States of America
91 90 89 88   5 4 3 2 1

Library of Congress Cataloging in Publication Data

Academic integrity and student development.

   (The Higher education administration series)
   Bibliography: p.
   1. Cheating (Education) 2. Students—United
States—Conduct of life. 3. Students—Legal
status, laws, etc.—United States.   I. Kibler,
William L.,   1954-   . II. Series.
IB3609.A28   1987   371.8'1   87-27667
ISBN 0-912557-08-7

The views expressed in this book are those of the individual
authors and are not necessarily those of College Administration
Publications, Inc.

This publication is designed to provide accurate and
authoritative information in regard to the subject matter
covered. It is sold with the understanding that the publisher is
not engaged in rendering legal, accounting or other professional
service. If legal advice or other expert assistance is required, the
services of a competent professional person should be sought.

—from a Declaration of Principles jointly adopted by a committee of the
American Bar Association and a committee of publishers.

Table of Contents

890177

Foreword

The pressure to make good grades is something all students live with in today's collegiate environment. Students compete for the highest grades to provide them with an edge in graduate and professional school admissions or in obtaining positions with the most prestigious companies. This pressure combined with the fact that most students attend college in order to be well off financially has created a stressful situation on many of our nation's campuses. Some students have responded to that stress by violating basic tenets of academic integrity. There is just so much at stake that cheating or other forms of academic dishonesty are seen as the only way out.

Colleges and universities must maintain their standards but they also have a responsibility to their students — those who are honest and those who are not. However, dealing with academic dishonesty raises many issues. Why do students cheat? What motivates them? Can we design programs to improve academic integrity? What about strategies to remove temptation other than lowering our standards? Will I be sued if I turn in a student? How should I go about reporting cheating? How should such offenses be handled after they are reported? Is academic dishonesty an academic offense or a disciplinary offense?

These and many other issues are addressed in this monograph in a practical and helpful style. The publication was primarily designed to assist students, faculty and administrators to understand the practical, legal and ethical parameters of academic integrity. The case studies which have been included are designed to be used with faculty orientation groups or as part of a staff development training program. There is also a model code to assist those institutions currently struggling with designing such a document. The model code is a unique contribution and incorporates many features of an honor system, and although it will not fit every situation, the document should at least provide a starting point for discussion.

Donald D. Gehring & D. Parker Young, *Series Editors*
January, 1988

About the Authors

WILLIAM L. KIBLER, Ed.S., is Associate Director of Student Affairs at Texas A&M University. He is responsible for supervising the student disciplinary system at Texas A&M and has worked extensively in the areas of student discipline/judicial affairs, academic dishonesty, and student legal issues for the past eight years at the University of Florida and Texas A&M University. Bill also has supervisory responsibilities in the areas of housing/residence life, orientation, and a myriad of other areas in student affairs at Texas A&M University. In addition, he has taught and co-taught courses in leadership, student development, and higher education administration at the University of Florida and Texas A&M University.

Mr. Kibler received his Bachelor of Arts, Master of Education and Specialist in Education degrees from the University of Florida. He is currently a candidate for a doctorate in higher education administration at Texas A&M University

ELIZABETH M. NUSS has served as a student affairs professional at the Pennsylvania State University, the University of Maryland, and most recently, as Dean for Undergraduate Life and Assistant Professor (part-time) at Indiana University. Effective July 1, 1987, she will become Executive Director of the National Association of Student Personnel Administrators (NASPA). Her professional interest is in student development theory, and in particular how student affairs practitioners can promote the ethical and moral development aspects of student life. She has made numerous presentations on topics of academic integrity, student development, professional ethics, and administrative problem-solving. Her dissertation, *Undergraduate Moral Development and Academic Dishonesty*, was selected as the 1982 NASPA Dissertation of the Year. She has published articles on academic integrity, financial management systems, and Japanese higher education.

BRENT G. PATERSON, Ph.D., is Supervisor of Student Judicial Affairs at Texas A&M University. He coordinates the administration of the student disciplinary system on this 36,000 student campus and serves as the University Disciplinary Hearing Officer. Prior to joining the staff at Texas A&M University, he held positions in residence life and admissions at the University of Denver and Lambuth College. In addition, he has taught classes in student personnel administration, counseling skills, and management at the University of Denver and Texas A&M University.

Dr. Paterson is a *cum laude* graduate of Lambuth College in Jackson, Tennessee. He holds a master's degree in student personnel services from Memphis State University and a doctorate in higher education administration from the University of Denver.

GARY PAVELA, J.D., is Director of Judicial Programs at the University of Maryland–College Park, where he also teaches courses in constitutional and administrative law. He is a member of the New York bar, has been a law clerk to a judge of the United States Court of Appeals for the Tenth Circuit, a fellow at the University of Wisconsin Center for Behavioral Science and Law, and a consultant to the Federal Judicial Center in Washington, D.C.

Mr. Pavela is a Phi Beta Kappa graduate of Lawrence College in Wisconsin, holds advanced degrees in history and in education from Wesleyan University in Connecticut, and a law degree from the University of Illinois. He has extensive experience in higher education administration, including positions in residence life, student services, academic affairs, and university legal counsel. His articles have appeared in the *Journal of College and University Law, The School Law Journal,* and *The Chronicle of Higher Education,* among others.

Chapter I

Academic Dishonesty—
A Contemporary Problem
In Higher Education

Elizabeth M. Nuss

This monograph is designed to provide guidance for colleges and universities interested in developing comprehensive programs to respond to academic integrity issues. This chapter defines academic dishonesty, provides a contemporary context for the issue, describes the scope of the problem, and considers the reasons why students cheat. Topics discussed in subsequent chapters include a discussion of student development theories, the implications of the theoretical framework for administrative and instructional practices, prevention strategies, and the legal issues associated with incidents of academic dishonesty.

WHAT IS ACADEMIC DISHONESTY?

One of the significant problems encountered in reviewing the research literature on academic dishonesty and cheating is the absence of a generally accepted definition. Academic dishonesty usually refers to forms of cheating and plagiarism which result in students giving or receiving unauthorized assistance in an academic exercise or receiving credit for work which is not their own. For the purposes of this monograph the definitions proposed by Pavela (1978, pp. 72-73) will be used. The definitions have been adopted by several colleges and universities including the University of Maryland and the University of Illinois. These include:

Cheating—intentionally using or attempting to use unauthorized materials, information, or study aids in any academic exercise. The term academic exercise includes all form of work submitted for credit or hours.

Fabrication—intentional and unauthorized falsification or invention of any information or citation in an academic exercise.

1

Facilitating academic dishonesty—intentionally or knowingly helping or attempting to help another to violate a provision of the institutional code of academic integrity.

Plagiarism—the deliberate adoption or reproduction of ideas or words or statements of another person as one's own without acknowledgment.

THE CONTEMPORARY CONTEXT

American higher education traditionally has viewed its role as encompassing more than just the acquisition of knowledge and the development of intellectual competence. Its goals generally have been described as helping students expand their knowledge and intellectual powers; to enhance students' moral, religious, and emotional interests and sensibilities; and to improve their performance in citizenship, work, family life, consumer choice, health, and other practical matters (Bowen, 1980). During the past twenty years student development theorists generally have agreed that the collegiate experience should enable students to mature and grow along several dimensions. These dimensions include: developing intellectual competence; learning to manage emotions; developing and establishing autonomy; establishing identity; developing interpersonal relationships; developing a sense of purpose; and developing integrity (Chickering, 1969). The manner in which colleges and universities have attempted to accomplish these goals and the individuals responsible have changed over the course of history (Sandeen, 1985).

Recent national attention has focused on how well higher education accomplishes its goals. Reports from the National Institute of Education (1984), The Association of American Colleges (1985), and The Newman Report (1985) raised questions about the quality of baccalaureate programs. These reports documented concern for the general condition of undergraduate programs and urged the academic community systematically to encourage integrity and coherence in undergraduate programs. Evidence has been cited which indicates that many college graduates are unable to perform fundamental tasks associated with effective communication, logical problem solving, persuasive argument, and critical analysis of data. Serious questions also have been raised about the ability of today's students to understand and appreciate complex societal problems many of which have an ethical component (Hesburgh, 1985). The questions and challenges raised by these reports are evidence that higher education is experiencing a confidence crisis. The trust and subsequent support American higher education has traditionally relied upon may be limited as its constituents—students, parents, legislators, alumni, and citizens—question the value of higher education. Reports of academic dishonesty and cheating contribute to this erosion of confidence and public support.

2

Academic dishonesty and cheating are not new issues for higher education. For the past fifty years the topic has been discussed on campuses and in the professional literature. Explanations as to why cheating occurs also have varied over time. In 1941, Drake concluded that the crux of the problem stemmed from competition for grades. More recently the Carnegie Council (1979) and others (Levine, 1980; Pavela, 1981) have indicated that today's students value achievement and the ability to compete successfully more than they value independent scholarship. The academic community has not been able to develop the intellectual values associated with effective scholarship in all of its students. These values have been described by Morrill (1980) as honesty, tolerance, respect, truth, rigor, and fairness.

HOW EXTENSIVE IS THE PROBLEM?

Acknowledging that we have not been successful in teaching today's students the values associated with effective scholarship raises an obvious question: Just how extensive is the problem of academic dishonesty? Most campuses have incidents of academic dishonesty. Whether or not the number of incidents is increasing is difficult to document. In 1979 a Carnegie Council study concluded that the percentage of students who reported that they had to cheat in order to get good grades increased from 7.5% in 1969 to 8.8% in 1976. At research universities the figures were even higher, increasing from 5.4% to 9.8% (Carnegie Council, 1979). Surveys at the University of Maryland, the University of Delaware, Arizona State University, and the University of California at Santa Barbara have found that over 25% of the students may have participated in some form of academic dishonesty at least once during their undergraduate experience. On the other hand, in 1981 Stanford University reported that the extent of cheating from 1961 to 1980 remained essentially stable. In 1985 however, alleged cheating by twenty-three students in an introductory psychology class resulted in the largest single honor code investigation in Stanford's history.

As mentioned earlier the difficulty in documenting academic dishonesty is complicated by the fact that there is not a common definition. Academic dishonesty is usually divided into four categories—cheating, fabrication, facilitating academic dishonesty, and plagiarism—with several behaviors associated with each category. Nuss (1981) found that students distinguished among dishonest behaviors and reported more frequent participation in behaviors considered to be among the least serious forms of academic dishonesty. Conversely students reported less frequent participation in the more serious forms. For example, "copying a few sentences without footnoting in a paper" and "working on homework with other students when it is not allowed" were the behaviors reported most frequently. Students reported

3

the least frequent participation in "taking an exam for another student" and "paying someone to write a paper to submit as your own work."

While there may be some debate over the precise dimensions of the problem it is agreed generally that academic dishonesty is a serious issue for all segments of higher education.

WHY STUDENTS CHEAT?

It is impossible to ascertain precisely what causes students to engage in academic dishonesty. Some contributing factors may have existed for generations while others may be unique to our current economic, political, and social setting. Research by Levine (1980) and Astin (1984) provide some useful insights. Societies go through periods of community and individual ascendancy (Levine, 1980). Community ascendancy is characterized by a future orientation, asceticism, concern for responsibility, and a duty to others. In contrast, individual ascendancy is characterized by a present orientation, hedonism, a concern for rights, and a duty to self. During periods of individual ascendancy general student character and values may be affected. Our current social, political, and economic circumstances are indicative of a period of individual ascendancy. Data collected on the attitudes and opinions of entering college freshmen (Astin, 1984) demonstrated a shift in student values and interests which might be characteristic of a period of individual ascendancy. For example, student endorsement of the value "being well off financially" has increased from 40% to 71%. Fifteen years ago the most popular student value was "developing a meaningful philosophy of life." Recently it ranked sixth (Freshman Characteristics, 1986) These shifts in values are not the cause of cheating but they are evidence that we are in a period of individual ascendancy—a time in which incidents of dishonesty may be more prevalent (Gehring, Nuss, & Pavela, 1986).

In a study at the University of Maryland, students were asked to select from several reasons why they are most likely to cheat (Nuss, 1981). Forty-five percent replied that students cheat in order to avoid failing the class and 21% indicated that the reason was because no one ever gets punished for it. Forty-eight percent indicated that the reason they personally would cheat is to avoid failing a class. Only 7% reported as a reason for their personal cheating that no one ever gets punished for it.

Gehring, Nuss & Pavela (1986) listed several factors which have been cited as contributing most frequently to incidents of academic dishonesty. Among those are the following:

- Students are unclear about what behaviors constitute academic dishonesty.
- Students believe that what they learn isn't relevant to their future career goals.

4

- Student values have changed. The ability to succeed at all costs is one of the most cherished values.
- Increased competition for enrollment in high demand disciplines and admission to prestigious graduate and professional schools prompt students to cheat to improve their grades, not just to avoid failure.
- Students are succumbing to frequent temptation. Examinations are not properly secured and faculty members are casual about proctoring exams. Assignments and examinations are repeated frequently from semester to semester.
- The risks associated with cheating are minimal. Students believe that no one gets punished and faculty members may avoid using campus disciplinary procedures by simply giving those suspected of cheating a lower or failing grade.

The academic community does not discuss the value it places on integrity. In one study approximately one-half of the faculty indicated that they never or rarely discuss university policies or their own requirements pertaining to academic dishonesty (Nuss, 1984). Without sufficient opportunities for discussion it is difficult, if not impossible, for new generations of college students to become aware of the values associated with effective scholarship.

SUMMARY

Academic dishonesty is a continuing problem for higher education. In the context of the contemporary economic, social, and political forces which impact higher education the problem takes on new significance. Institutions of higher education must inspire and renew the confidence of those constituents they depend upon for support. Higher education must prepare citizens and leaders able to confront the complex social problems of our times. Students must be capable of recognizing and dealing with ethical dilemmas that arise among or from organizational pressures, conflicts of interest, competition among multiple goods and consequences, and ordinary human weakness (Andrews, 1985).

Colleges and universities that decide to confront academic dishonesty have an excellent opportunity to teach the values associated with effective scholarship and to help prepare students to respond to other ethical dilemmas. The time and energy needed to develop a systematic approach to addressing a current campus problem may have long-term positive implications for the institution. These college graduates may be among the few with the experience necessary to respond to the complex ethical and social dilemmas confronting our society.

Chapter II

Student Development Perspectives
On Academic Integrity

Elizabeth M. Nuss

A frequent criticism directed at academic administrators is that their practice is seldom guided by theoretical constructs. This chapter has been designed to help academic administrators consider how an understanding of student development and moral development theory might help to improve the quality of academic integrity on their campuses. Thus, a review of student development and moral development literature has been included. A primary goal in preparing this chapter has been to achieve the appropriate balance between theory and practical information for a diverse audience. Hopefully the material in this chapter will be viewed as an adequate introduction for those practitioners not familiar with the student development literature and yet will still be considered a useful review for those practitioners conversant with the literature. The chapter provides a brief overview of the student development literature focusing on moral development, explores the relationship between moral reasoning and ethical behavior, and considers the practical implications of the theoretical framework.

THEORETICAL OVERVIEW

The principles of student development are useful tools for colleges and universities as they design educational programs and activities to alleviate academic dishonesty and to teach students the fundamental values associated with effective scholarship. Nevitt Sanford (1962) and others encouraged us to become concerned with educating the "whole person." Sanford argued that the college environment should enable the student to encounter the appropriate challenges and support for development (Sanford, 1966; Sanford and Axelrod, 1979). As the result of efforts to identify elements of the collegiate experience and the college environment which contributed to the education of the whole student, a body of research and theory evolved which describes the way adolescents mature and develop into adulthood.

7

Knefelkamp, Widick, and Parker (1978) made a significant contribution by categorizing the existing theories. The five categories were described as the psycho-social theories, cognitive developmental theories, maturity models, typology models, and person-environment interaction models. All five groups of theorists, albeit in somewhat different ways, focused on the importance of the interaction of the individual with the environment and the fact that various characteristics or aspects of the environment serve as sources of challenge and support which facilitate development. The work of the cognitive developmental theorists is particularly relevant to academic integrity because it focuses on how individuals reason about ethical and moral dilemmas. For the purposes of our discussion we will utilize the cognitive developmental approach to moral development as the theoretical framework.

The current moral development research began in 1955 with Lawrence Kohlberg's dissertation research. The early cognitive developmental research viewed moral development as an invariant, hierarchical, and sequential movement through a series of qualitatively different stages of moral reasoning. Stages of moral development were the structures of thought which underlay the moral judgments. Cognitive developmental theorists focused on the intellectual process used by the individual rather than on the content of the thought.

Other scholars working with Kohlberg (Turiel, 1966; Kohlberg & Kramer, 1969; Krebs, 1967; Rest, 1979, and Gilligan, 1982) contributed significant research which confirmed some aspects of the model and suggested new directions and perspectives. Gilligan's work (1982) focused on the apparent differences between the reasoning of men and women. She argued that the stage theory view of moral maturity was flawed because the early research was conducted with male subjects and therefore neglected the views of female subjects. Based on her research with women she argued that a more adequate representation of moral maturity should recognize distinctions between the ethic of justice and the ethic of care. The ethic of justice views rights and responsibilities from the perspective that everyone should be treated equally while the ethic of care is based on the premise that no one should be hurt. Rest's research (1983 & 1985) provided helpful perspectives about the relationship between moral reasoning and the production of moral behavior.

PRINCIPLES OF MORAL DEVELOPMENT THEORY

While researchers may differ in their views of the stage theory, particularly as experienced by men and women, there tends to be general agreement on certain principles. Based on recent empirical findings Rest, (1983) argued that development needs to be considered in more complex terms than simply the picture of an individual as being in one stage and moving step by step through a series of stages. Development is viewed as the gradual shifting from the use of lower stages to higher stages. "Development is portrayed in terms of the progressive understanding of the cooperative relationships, how rights and duties are balanced, and the conditions that sustain the cooperative schemes" (Rest, 1983, p. 587). *Table 1* describes the stages of moral judgment which illustrate the views of cooperative relationships. The principles of moral development theory are summarized as follows:

1. Development is viewed as the gradual shifting from the use of lower stages to higher stages.
2. Development is portrayed in terms of the progressive understanding of cooperative relationships.
3. Development of moral judgment requires more than just the attainment of certain rational operations.
4. Development is determined by the experiences and stimuli which result from the interaction between the individual and the environment.
5. Development requires a variety of social experiences including an opportunity to encounter different perspectives and roles. Development requires moral conflict in order for the individual to recognize the inadequacy of lower stages of reasoning.

TABLE I. — KOHLBERG'S MORAL JUDGMENT STAGES

Level and Stage	Content of Stage		Social Perspective of Stage
	What is Right	Reasons for Doing Right	
LEVEL I—PRECONVENTIONAL **Stage I—Heteronomous Morality**	To avoid breaking rules backed by punishment, obedience for its own sake, and avoiding physical damage to persons and property.	Avoidance of punishment, and the superior power of authorities.	*Egocentric point of view.* Doesn't consider the interests of others or recognize that they differ from the actor's; doesn't relate two points of view. Actions are considered physically rather than in terms of psychological interests of others. Confusion of authority's perspective with one's own.
Stage 2—Individualism, Instrumental Purpose, and Exchange	Following rules only when it is to someone's immediate interest; acting to meet one's own interests and needs and letting others do the same. Right is also what's fair, what's an equal exchange, a deal, an agreement.	To serve one's own needs or interests in a world where you have to recognize that other people have their interests too.	*Concrete individualistic perspective.* Aware that everybody has his own interest to pursue and these conflict so that right is relative (in the concrete individualistic sense).

NOTE: From Kohlberg, L. Moral stages and moralization: The cognitive development approach. In T. Lickona (Ed.) *Moral Development and Behavior* (pp. 34-35), 1976, New York: Holt, Rinehart and Winston. Copyright by T. Lickona. Reprinted by permission.

Level and Stage	Content of Stage		Social Perspective of Stage
	What is Right	*Reasons for Doing Right*	
LEVEL II—CONVENTIONAL **Stage 3—Mutual Interpersonal Expectations, Relationships, and Interpersonal Conformity**	Living up to what is expected by people close to you or what people generally expect of people in your role as son, brother, friend, etc. "Being good" is important and means having good motives, showing concern about others. It also means keeping mutual relationships, such as trust, loyalty, respect, and gratitude.	The need to be a good person in your own eyes and those of others. Your caring for others. Belief in the Golden Rule. Desire to maintain rules and authority which support stereotypical good behavior.	*Perspective of the individual in relationships with other individuals.* Aware of shared feelings, agreements, and expectations which take primacy over individual interests. Relates points of view through the concrete Golden Rule, putting yourself in the other guy's shoes. Does not yet consider generalized system perspective.
Stage 4—Social System and Conscience	Fulfilling the actual duties to which you have agreed. Laws are to be upheld except in extreme cases where they conflict with other fixed social duties. Right is also contributing to society, the group, or institution.	To keep the institution going as a whole, to avoid the breakdown in the system "if everyone did it," or the imperative of conscience to meet one's defined obligations (easily confused with Stage 3 belief in rules and authority).	*Differentiates societal point of view from interpersonal agreement or motives.* Takes the point of view of the system that defines roles and rules. Considers individual relations in terms of place in the system.

11

Level and Stage	Content of Stage		Social Perspective of Stage
	What is Right	Reasons for Doing Right	
LEVEL III—POSTCONVENTIONAL or PRINCIPLED **Stage 5—Social Contract or Utility and Individual Rights**	Being aware that people hold a variety of values and opinions, that most values and rules are relative to your group. These relative rules should usually be upheld, however, in the interest of impartiality and because they are the social contract. Some nonrelative values and rights like *life* and *liberty*, however, must be upheld in any society and regardless of majority opinion.	A sense of obligation to law because of one's social contract to make & abide by laws for welfare of all, for the protection of all people's rights. A feeling of contractual commitment, freely entered upon, to family, friendship, trust, and work obligations. Concern that laws and duties be based on rational calculation of overall utility, "the greatest good for the greatest number."	*Prior-to-society perspective.* Perspective of a rational individual aware of values and rights prior to social attachments and contracts. Integrates perspectives by formal mechanisms of agreement, contract, objective impartiality, and due process. Considers moral and legal points of view; recognizes that they sometimes conflict and finds it difficult to integrate them.
Stage 6—Universal Ethical Principles	Following self-chosen ethical principles. Particular laws or social agreements are usually valid because they rest on such principles. When laws violate these principles, one acts in accordance with the principle. Principles are universal principles of justice: the equality of human rights and respect for the dignity of human beings as individuals.	The belief as a rational person in the validity of universal moral principles and a sense of personal commitment to them.	*Perspective of a moral point of view from which social arrangements derive.* Perspective is that of any rational individual recognizing the nature of morality or the fact that persons are ends in themselves and must be treated as such.

THE RELATIONSHIP BETWEEN
MORAL REASONING AND BEHAVIOR

In a discussion about ways in which colleges and universities can enhance academic integrity it is important to consider the relationship between stages of moral reasoning and moral behavior.

The research reviewed by Nuss (1981) demonstrated that moral judgment is not synonymous with moral action. Kohlberg (1971) considered moral judgment to be a necessary if not sufficient condition for moral action. He also argued that moral judgment is the only distinctively moral factor in moral behavior (1975). Rest (1979) stated, "Moral judgment as a psychological variable has a limited role in the explanation of moral action—it may be a star role but it is only one player in a large cast" (p. 170).

The relationships between moral reasoning, moral behavior, and the particular situation are complex. The research appears to support the following generalizations (Boyce and Jensen, 1978, p. 119):

- persons operating at higher stages of moral judgment tend to act with greater consistency in their judgments;
- there is a relationship between moral judgments, beliefs, values, and behavior;
- changes through persuasion or verbal interaction can influence behavior; and
- the stage of the message is important in determining the amount of behavioral change that occurs.

Hersh, Paolitto, and Reimer (1979) cautioned against attempting to generalize from studies with relatively straight-forward choice situations, such as cheating studies, to behavior in less structured decision making situations. They argued that the particular setting plays an important role in promoting consistency between judgment and action.

Rest (1983 & 1985) proposed a four-part framework to consider the production of moral behavior and action in a particular situation. The four component processes are briefly described as follows:

Component I Moral Sensitivity. This process involves the interpretation of the situation and identification of possible courses of action. Research findings on Component I indicate that many people have difficulty in interpreting even relatively simple situations; striking individual differences exist among people in their sensitivity to the needs of other; and the capacity to make these inferences generally develops with age (Rest, 1983, p.559).

Component II Moral Judgment. When the alternative courses of action have been identified, the individual must be able to determine the moral ideal. The cognitive developmental research on moral reasoning focuses primarily on this component, how does the individual reason about the moral alternatives? Can the individual identify the moral alternative?

Component III Moral Motivation. The moral course of action has been identified, but the individual must choose it over the alternative courses of action. This process involves prioritizing the values associated with the particular situation in such a manner so that the moral value is placed higher than other competing values such as affiliation, success, security, etc.

Component IV Moral Behavior. This process involves executing and implementing a plan of action which results in the moral behavior. Having placed the moral alternative ahead of the other options the individual must be able to keep the goal in sight, have sufficient ego-strength to tolerate frustration, lack of support or cooperation, and other hurdles.

Rest's model makes it apparent that if colleges and universities are interested in fostering academic integrity among their students a carefully developed and comprehensive set of educational programs, policies, and procedures is necessary. Rest (1985) argued that "educational interventions aimed at moral development must recognize the multifaceted complexity of the process involved in morality (p. 77)." Consequently, the assessment of the impact of an educational program upon moral development must take into account the complexities of morality.

Lets consider a hypothetical cheating situation.

Three friends, John, Susan, and David are preparing for a comprehensive final examination in accounting. Susan and David are aware that in previous years copies of the final have been "acquired" prior to the exam and were available for sale to certain students. According to campus folklore and tradition the exam is only sold to those students who have been 'crafty' enough to find a way to identify the 'salesperson' and to convince that individual that they can be trusted enough to purchase the exam. Susan and David are intrigued by the idea of solving this puzzle and approach John with the suggestion that rather than study for the exam they should attempt to buy the exam. Acquiring the examination is viewed by the two students to be as much of a test of their problem-solving abilities as successfully completing the examination.

In this context, students must be able to interpret the situation. Can the students identify the significant and responsible actors in the situation? Do the students recognize the competing pressures? Can the students identify multiple courses of action? Assuming that the students recognize the several courses of action available to them, do the students recognize alternatives that are considered to be the morally correct option(s)? Recognizing the moral course(s) of action, will the students choose to pursue it? Or, will the achievement motive or the need for peer support and affiliation be a higher priority than the value for honesty?

Let's assume the students have interpreted the situation as one involving academic dishonesty and recognize that they have several options available. They can decide to participate; decide not to participate but not interfere with the planned activity; try to stop the violation from occurring; report the incident and those individuals associated with it to the faculty; or possibly develop some combination of these alternatives. John decides not to participate and informs the other students that "should they decide to continue with the cheating scheme he will report them to the faculty member." John is willing to risk the rejection of friends and possibly a lower grade on the exam in order to do the right thing. Will John have the inner strength to persist in this decision and actually execute the behavior in spite of the harassment and threats received from Susan and David?

If colleges and universities are serious about addressing the problem of academic dishonesty, they must design programs, policies, and procedures which help their students respond to ethical dilemmas similar to this one. In the next section some practical approaches will be discussed.

PRACTICAL IMPLICATIONS OF THE THEORETICAL FRAMEWORK

We have argued in the previous chapter that even though the precise causes of academic dishonesty were unclear and the extent of the problem was unknown, colleges and universities needed to initiate systematic and conscientious efforts to help students appreciate the fundamental values associated with effective scholarship and to embrace the standards of academic integrity.

The case cited above is only one example of the ethical dilemmas students face. It is incumbent upon students, faculty, and administrators to design ways to help students respond to these situations. While each campus has its own unique mission and value system, it is safe to conclude that all institutions agree on the necessity for academic integrity. The student development theoretical framework provides guidance for the design of proposed approaches to the problem. The assumptions include (Nuss, 1981):

1. College students are at different places developmentally and should not be considered as a homogeneous group.
2. Moral development is facilitated by opportunities to role play, confront different social or moral perspectives, and participate in decision making on ethical issues.

15

3. Students can comprehend moral reasoning that is related to their own stages of moral reasoning, but are unable to comprehend moral reasoning that is more than one stage above their own.
4. The environment should provide the necessary challenges and support to encourage new responses and developmental growth.
5. The moral development of some students may exceed that of some faculty and staff.
6. Different educational approaches and initiatives can contribute to different aspects of moral development (Dalton, Healy, & Moore, 1985).
7. Educational interventions and programs must consider the four component processes and the complexities of moral behavior (Rest, 1985).

The effectiveness of the measures which colleges and universities take to enhance academic integrity can be improved if they are planned within the context of moral development theory. The Carnegie Council and others have recommended specific steps colleges and universities should take (Carnegie Council, 1979; Levine, 1980; & Pavela, 1981). For illustrative purposes, several of these steps will be discussed within the context of the developmental framework. These include the importance of a clearly written policy, opportunities for discussion and dialogue, equitable adjudication procedures, the role of sanctions, and the importance of instructional settings.

The student development literature emphasizes the important role that the environment plays in fostering development. Clearly communicating the community's expectations for academic integrity is one important way for the environment to foster student development. Institutional policies and expectations should include definitions of academic dishonesty, examples of behaviors which constitute infractions, a description of the process followed when alleged violations occur, and a description of the sanctions usually imposed. The literature indicates that students are at different places developmentally and that development is facilitated by opportunities to role play and confront different social and moral perspectives. How many of our campuses provide sufficient opportunities for discussion about the academic integrity standards and the policies among faculty and students? Too often the policy is published in official university publications, but very seldom is there active discussion and dialogue. Frequent discussions about academic integrity provide the institution with an opportunity to communicate the value it places on integrity relative to other values such as achievement and competition. While each campus can best determine when and how these discussions should take place, consideration should be given to incorporating discussions into orientation programs, learning skills classes, and during the first meeting of every course. With this approach, students have an opportunity to seek clarification or elaboration and could become familiar with the way different disciplines or professions view integrity and ethical questions. The discussions may help students avoid unintentional violations as a result of ignorance or misunderstanding. The variety of approaches also improves the likelihood that programs will have an impact on students who are reasoning at different developmental stages.

Another area that should be considered within the context of the theoretical framework is the development of equitable procedures for resolving cases of alleged academic dishonesty. The procedures should be compatible with the institutional mission and the needs of the campus community and ensure due process for all parties. The procedures should be fair and not so cumbersome that faculty members are discouraged from using them. Campus procedures should provide the student with an opportunity to confront the ethical implications of their behavior, gain a better understanding of the roles and responsibilities of students and faculty within the academic community, develop an appreciation of the values associated with effective scholarship, and gain exposure to forms of moral reasoning they can comprehend and which are likely to stimulate their development.

The role that sanctions and the disciplinary processes play also should be considered within the context of the student development framework. Pavela (1981) argued effectively against the practice of simply giving a student a failing grade for several reasons. The practice does not serve as a deterrent to students already in jeopardy of failing and it misleads other schools to which the students may apply. Most importantly, the practice deprives the student of an adequate opportunity to confront the ethical implications of the behavior. The imposition of strict sanctions is not antithetical to student development. Consistently-applied sanctions represent the essence of challenge and support. It is essential that faculty members reach agreement on appropriate sanctions for particular types of offenses. If faculty believe the sanctions imposed are too extreme, they may be reluctant to report suspected violations (Barnett & Dalton, 1981). In order to inform both students and faculty about the types of violations occurring on campus and the typical sanctions imposed, institutions should consider publishing periodic reports summarizing reported violations and subsequent action taken. The published reports should not include the name of the involved student, but should identify the academic department or school.

To facilitate the moral development of students, the actions of the academic community must be consistent with its published statements and policies. Conditions which facilitate academic dishonesty and failure to insist that faculty members demonstrate high ethical standards communicates a mixed message to students and creates an

17

Chapter III

Strategies to Prevent Academic Dishonesty

William L. Kibler
Brent G. Paterson

INTRODUCTION

Chapters I and II have stressed the importance of understanding academic dishonesty as a problem and understanding why many students resort to what many would consider a drastic measure. Chapters IV addresses legal issues and administrative procedures related to the resolution of academic dishonesty cases. This chapter discusses the importance of prevention in dealing with academic dishonesty, the responsibility for prevention and suggested strategies. At the conclusion of this chapter is a chart summarizing dishonesty detection and prevention strategies.

The best way to deal with academic dishonesty is to prevent it from happening in the first place. This is no easy task, but it is a manageable responsibility and it begins long before the first day of class. Understanding the issues involved in academic dishonesty is a prerequisite to planning effective prevention strategies. The discussion that follows will address how to implement an overall prevention strategy on the first day of class and how to follow through with the strategy to establish the appropriate atmosphere in the course. Emphasis will be on strategies for different types of tests and assignments. Although we will recommend methods and strategies which may seem tedious, it is important to remember that the time spent preventing academic dishonesty is minimal in comparison to the amount of time that could be spent involved in handling one or more cases of cheating.

As you read this chapter, keep in mind that it is not assumed that all students cheat or will attempt to cheat. Most students possess the integrity and moral reasoning to understand that cheating is not appropriate. Faculty members and administrators should attempt to limit opportunities for cheating by incorporating prevention strategies that are in agreement with individual teaching style and methods. The broad array of prevention strategies presented in this chapter may be considered a resource for formulating individual classroom or institutional prevention strategies.

WHO'S RESPONSIBLE?

In Chapter I, Nuss described some of the possible causes of academic dishonesty, thus placing the responsibility for prevention on many individuals. Houston (1976b) suggested that budget limitations force multiple choice tests to be given in crowded classrooms with an inadequate number of proctors. When the pressure to obtain high grades was combined with these conditions, he maintained that the absence of apprehension of cheaters can be understood. Other researchers, Boodish (1962), Montor (1971), and Uhlig and Howes (1967), for example, proposed that a student's morality is related to cheating. In Chapter II, Nuss discussed the relationship between moral reasoning and behavior. Vitro (1971) found that cheaters experienced parental discipline at either end of the continuum (i.e. harsh physical punishment or minimal nonpunitive discipline). Even the increased commercialization in higher education has been viewed as a cause for student unethical behavior (David and Kovach, 1979).

While the causes of academic dishonesty may be uncertain, it is clear that everyone is responsible for the prevention of academic dishonesty. The responsibility should be collectively assumed by students, their parents, faculty members, academic advisors, administrators, and the institutions themselves. The values instilled in individuals by their parents will influence the choices they make during the college years. The institution has the responsibility to define academic dishonesty and establish a learning environment in which integrity is valued. Strategies to prevent academic dishonesty at the institutional level will be examined later in this chapter.

FACULTY RESPONSIBILITY

Much of the responsibility to prevent academic dishonesty has traditionally fallen on the instructor. Singhal and Johnson (1983) stated, "The prevention of academic dishonesty is one of the basic responsibilities of the professor" (p. 13). According to Evett (1980) the responsibility should be approached as a privilege rather than a task. The professor needs to develop a plan to deter, detect, and prosecute cheating (Singhal and Johnson). Such a plan includes establishing a classroom atmosphere that deters cheating as well as developing strategies to prevent cheating on tests and plagiarism.

STUDENT RESPONSIBILITY

The student's responsibility can be viewed in two ways. First, students who are inclined to cheat must accept responsibility for their behavior. Students have chosen to enter into a community of learning. When in this community, they must abide by the accepted norms of behavior. Most institutions of higher learning do not tolerate those who cheat. Beyond the collegial community, students should view the expectations of society and attempt to live within them. Students are depriving themselves of an opportunity to gain knowledge that may be beneficial in the future. Students also may be forming standards of behavior which may lead to unethical conduct in other areas. Second, students who have knowledge that cheating is occurring have the responsibility to report it. Whether or not to report an incident of academic dishonesty can be a dilemma for students, and they must decide how to handle the situation within their own moral framework. Honor codes at many institutions expect students to report incidents of academic dishonesty.

HONOR CODES

A number of institutions, such as the U.S. Military Academy, Stanford University, and the University of Virginia, have relied upon honor codes for years. Under these systems, students pledge to refrain from cheating and agree to report violations by others. Strict honor guidelines often require the automatic dismissal of first-time offenders. The major criticism of honor systems is that cheating often continues unabated in unproctored test situations and that most students are too reticent to inform on their classmates (Hardy, 1982).

As a result of these realities, several institutions, including the University of Florida and Johns Hopkins University, have abandoned their honor codes in recent years and substituted proctor systems (Stone, 1977). Leming's (1978) study found that students are significantly more likely to cheat under situations of low-supervision than under situations of high-supervision. Similarly, Williams (1969) found that over ninety percent of the students at Huntington College who were exposed to both systems agreed that the proctor system discouraged cheating much more than the honor system. Based upon these insights the Model Code of Academic Integrity (Appendix II) retains a proctor system, while incorporating the more viable components of a traditional honor code.

PREVENTION STRATEGIES

Institutional Level

The prevention of academic dishonesty at the classroom level is much easier to manage if the institution is committed to addressing cheating as a major problem and is committed to taking measures at the institutional level to prevent it. Such institutional commitment is essential to the establishment of sound and consistent prevention strategies in the classroom. What follows is an outline of institutional measures which are suggested to establish an institutional commitment to prevent cheating:

1. Statement regarding academic dishonesty. The institution should issue a very clear, strongly worded statement indicating that academic dishonesty is unacceptable. This statement should be printed in all relevant institutional documents, such as the catalog, student handbook, faculty handbook, and every issue of the schedule of classes. It should be integrated into the syllabus of every course.

2. Establish a code of conduct for academic dishonesty. Pavela develops a complete model code in Appendix II. The code adopted by the institution should accomplish at least three goals:

    a. Clearly define academic dishonesty in language that is clear to all students and faculty and yet general enough to apply to the many different courses.

    b. Establish an understandable and workable process for handling cheating when it does occur.

    c. Define sanctions that may be implemented for academic dishonesty and clarify who has the authority to impose them.

3. Integrate orientation regarding academic dishonesty into new student orientation programs for freshmen, transfer students, and graduate students. Residence hall counselors and peer counselors also should receive training in this area.

4. Training for faculty and graduate teaching assistants. This should begin with a comprehensive manual which provides practical guidelines for faculty and teaching assistants on the prevention of academic dishonesty. This manual should be distributed annually. Faculty and teaching assistants should receive training in the following areas:

    a. Definition of academic dishonesty.

    b. Prevention strategies which can and should be used in the classroom. This should include setting the appropriate atmosphere in the class, proctoring exams in effective, but inobtrusive ways, and detecting cheating when it occurs.

    c. Process for handling cheating cases.

    d. Sanctions.

The approach the institution takes toward the problem of academic dishonesty can have a significant impact on the attitude of the faculty toward cheating. A positive, proactive approach by the institution should help foster that attitude among the faculty. However, if the institution chooses to ignore or deny the problem, it serves to perpetuate the attitude discussed by Hardy (1982):

> There are countless professors who refuse to address the problem of academic dishonesty. Some professors try to minimize the prob-

lem for fear that it may reflect badly on their ability to teach. Young professors especially eschew drawing attention to cheating in their classrooms because it might reveal to their department chairperson that they lack the requisite skills or experience to avert such infractions. Still others do not like to report cheating because they do not want to be branded as "zealots" or "troublemakers" by their colleagues or students. The biggest problem, however, is that many simply deny that such problems exist . . . Such naivete not only encourages cheating, but is entirely out of touch with reality. (p. 70)

The attitude of the individual faculty member greatly influences the atmosphere in the classroom toward cheating, which is the next topic.

Classroom Atmosphere

A positive classroom atmosphere helps prevent cheating. The atmosphere need not be one of total trust. Tittle and Rowe (1974) found that under conditions of trust, the level of cheating was very high. Their research indicated that moral appeals had no effect on the incidence of cheating. The data they obtained disclosed that cheating can be reduced by a threat of being caught and punished. These results may be explained by the moral maturity of the students in the study. Likewise, Singhal and Johnson (1983) stated, "A key aspect in the prevention of cheating is setting an academic atmosphere where honesty is an expected standard and any deviation from this standard can be readily detected and handled" (p. 15).

At the first class meeting, teachers should present their expectations. The presentation should consist of a clear definition of cheating to include group work, tests, and plagiarism. Students should be informed of their moral responsibilities and institutional honor codes and ethics. Penalties for failure to comply with the expectations should be stated clearly and placed in the course syllabus.

Studies have found that the personality and teaching styles of the professor may influence cheating behavior (Bushway and Nash, 1977). Shirk and Hoffman (1961) proposed a theory that very authoritarian professors incite cheating. Their authoritarian professor was characterized as one who informs the students that they are inferior for not knowing all the answers and the test grades reflect their intellectual abilities. Research by Steininger, Johnson, and Kirts (1964) seemed to support this belief. They suggested that teachers who give excessively difficult tests may create an increase in cheating. Woods' study cited in Bushway and Nash reported that cheating may be encouraged inadvertently by teachers who are too easy or too hard.

Singhal and Johnson (1983) promoted the following steps to prevent academic dishonesty:

1. A clear statement of student moral responsibilities and penalties for violations should be made.

2. Provide equal access to study materials.
3. The effects of grades for activities that cannot be closely controlled should be minimized.
4. Course requirements should be challenging but not overwhelming.
5. Structure exams in a way to prevent cheating.
6. Make copying, plagiarism, and other forms of cheating difficult by paying attention to security situations. (p. 14)

Testing

Cheating on tests can be prevented or minimized if the teacher takes the necessary precautions. These precautions must be taken at all stages of the testing process—test preparation, test administration, test grading, and the recording of grades. Students have taken advantage of opportunities to cheat in every stage.

Some of the research seems to suggest that the level of cheating on tests may be affected by the level of anxiety of the students. If the anxiety levels are reduced, less cheating will occur (Mueller, 1953; Parrott, 1972; Singhal and Johnson, 1983; Weber, McBee, and Krebs, 1983). These authors recommended some ways to lower test anxiety. One way to minimize anxiety is to give frequent tests or graded assignments (Mueller). By giving frequent tests, the final grade will not depend largely upon one or two exams. Parrott suggested that students be provided with study questions in advance from which questions for the test will be selected. For objective tests, Parrott advocated placing exam questions on reserve in the library. The test could then contain the same questions arranged in a different order. Also, a review session can be held prior to the test, perhaps the class period before (Mueller; Parrott). Students should not expect a summary of the material covered. Rather, they should be encouraged to be prepared to ask questions in order to clarify areas of confusion. Why reduce test anxiety? Students will learn more when given direction of what material is important. Also, the student who does not know what to expect on a test may panic and view cheating as the only way to obtain a good grade.

The preparation of a test is important in the prevention of academic dishonesty. The teacher must decide upon the type of test to be given. Tests may be structured so that cheating is unlikely. For example, a graduate professor at the University of Denver would give his class an article to read. The test would consist of a few questions concerning the article. The students were expected to respond to the questions concerning the article in relation to the material covered in the class. Students were permitted to use books, journals, and notes, so long as they were footnoted. A typical response would be three to five written pages. If proper security precautions are taken to insure no student has access to the questions prior to the test, it is virtually impossible to cheat on this type of test.

Tests like the one described above cannot be widely used since large classes make essay tests too difficult and time-consuming to grade. As an alternative to essay tests, teachers often use multiple choice tests and short answer tests. Large lecture classes in which multiple choice or short answer tests are administered make cheating a low-risk proposition (Hardy, 1982). Randy Herbertson, a former student body president at the University of Colorado said, "When there are five hundred kids in a lecture hall, if you look up from your paper, you're a cheater. The answers flow right down the aisles" (Wellborn, 1980, p. 39).

To help prevent cheating on multiple choice and short answer tests, special care needs to be taken in test preparation. First, be sure that you construct a new test. Various student organizations are well known for their test files. Whether obtained legally or otherwise, there are probably several copies of a professor's tests from the past few years available on campus. Second, alternate test forms should be created and distributed in each class. The test form should be easily distinguishable to the person distributing and grading the tests. However, it need not be obvious to the students. One author suggested using different color paper for different forms. While this provides easy identification for the professor it also allows the student cheater to seek out another test of the same color from which to copy. One suggestion is to use a computer to scramble test questions and create the grading sheets. In a small class, each student might have a different test form.

The major objection to take-home tests and open-book tests has been that they provide greater opportunities to cheat. Research by Weber et al (1983) suggested, however, that cheating on take-home tests is not any greater than on closed- or open-book tests. It should be noted these findings are inconsistent with the findings of Nuss and other researchers. Although, reduced stress in open-book tests compared with closed-book tests may lead to less cheating. No matter what type of test is selected, the exam questions should fit the material covered (Mueller, 1953).

Test Preparation

Additional security precautions should be taken when preparing a test. The availability of the prepared test must be guarded. Tests left lying around the office are too accessible to student workers and visiting students. When a word processor is used to produce the test, do not leave it on the computer. If possible, put it on a disc which can be taken home or locked up when not needed. There is no reason to tempt a student. In addition, a statement of the class policy concerning academic dishonesty, including the consequences for being guilty of an offense, should be placed on each test. Paper should be provided for the test and any scratch work. Singhal and Johnson (1983) recommended that scratch paper and answer sheets be bound or stapled prior to distribution to students. The answer sheet should be stapled on the back and students instructed not to tear it off. This causes the students some inconvenience, since they must continually turn pages, but it forces them to keep their answer sheets covered. It is also a good idea to use a pre-coded or pre-marked answer sheet where the students simply circle or fill in the correct responses, instead of an answer sheet with spaces where students write in the correct answer. This lessens the risk of changing answers when the exam is handed back for review. For example, a "c" could be changed to a "d" with a simple stroke of the pen (Hardy, 1982). If blue books are to be used and are not provided, require students to turn in blank ones at the class period prior to the test. The books can then be distributed at the start of the test (Fagan, 1984). Taking these security precautions will reduce cheating. Also, instructors may have special methods that meet their needs.

Test Administration

John Houston of the University of California, Los Angeles, has written many articles concerning techniques designed to minimize answer copying. His research showed that significant copying occurs when every seat in the classroom is filled and only one test form is used. This cheating usually occurred between the cheater and the person on either side (Houston, 1976b). When spaced seating was assigned on a random basis so that every other column of seats was empty, there was a significant decrease in the amount of answer copying (Houston, 1976a). Random or instructor arranged seating is important to prevent students from taking prearranged seats within line of sight of another student's test.

Each test should be numbered prior to distribution. In fact, Hardy (1982) suggested that after the tests are typed, duplicated, and collated, they should be numbered sequentially and filed securely, preferably at home. This method guards against students burglarizing the office and escaping with a test or an employee being bribed to steal a test. Following a test, the proctor should make sure all tests have been returned. A "stooge," possibly hired by others, may sit in on the exam just for the purpose of stealing a copy of it for others (Hardy, 1982). If the test is to be given to another class, copies of the lifted test will be distributed quickly. If the test will not be given to another class, it will be filed by the individuals or a group for future reference. By numbering the tests, one can determine easily the number of tests distributed and the number returned.

The method of collecting completed tests is important. Each student must hand in the test personally. When handing the test to the instructor, students must show their picture ID. The instructor, having inspected the ID, then initials the test. This method prevents "ringers" from taking tests for other students. However, there is one problem. The instructor does not know which students were "neighbors" during the test, making it difficult to determine if copying occurred. Singhal and Johnson (1983) suggested a method for determining "neighbor cheating." They believed that tests should be left on the student's desk. The tests are picked up in sequence after the students have left. The tests are then graded one question at a time. Patterns should emerge if cheating occurred. To eliminate the "ringer," Singhal and Johnson (1983) have students display their ID's on their desks. The instructor then walks through the room checking to verify that a student has not taken the place of another student.

The instructor or individual proctoring the exam should be trained in methods to prevent cheating during a test and the procedures to be followed if someone is suspected of cheating. The methods presented in this chapter should be helpful to proctors. Additional methods of prevention include making sure all books and packs are properly stowed under the seats or placed in front of the classroom and no communication is permitted. Instructors should be present during all in-class exams. Remember, one of the most effective methods to deter cheating is proctoring (Houston, 1976a; Singhal and Johnson, 1983; Fagan, 1984).

After the Test

Security following the test is just as important as prior to the test. The possibility of burglary of an office should not be ignored. At one institution it was discovered that a student left a classroom with a test, took it home, completed the test, then bribed an employee to allow him to enter the instructor's office. Fortunately, an alert instructor detected the "newly arrived test" in the pile of tests on his desk the next day. Lock tests away in a safe place!

Preventing cheating on tests requires an effort by the instructor, but this effort may promote greater learning by students. In addition, the effort displays the instructor's commitment to prevent academic dishonesty. If a student alleged to have cheated on an exam wishes to challenge the professor, having a plan for prevention and following it will enhance the professor's case. However, the instructor should not become complacent. Students who engage in academic dishonesty can be creative, and will find new ways to "beat the system."

Plagiarism

Plagiarism can be widespread, yet is often hard to detect, largely because it is difficult to agree on exactly what constitutes plagiarism. It is important that plagiarism be clearly defined in the institution's conduct code (a definition of plagiarism appears in the model code in Appendix II). If not, it is advisable that the instructor specify what will constitute plagiarism in the particular course.

The stakes for plagiarism are as high as those in tests, often higher. They can include the high value of the paper relative to the final course grade, the completion of a requirement in which one lacks aptitude, impersonal conditions in basic writing courses, faculty detachment from the teaching of fundamental writing skills, and the plethora of potential sources that could be copied (Fagan, 1984).

The dilemma of trying to maintain a balance between employing effective techniques for prevention of cheating, yet not inhibiting the effectiveness of student learning is most difficult when combatting plagiarism. The best guard against plagiarism seems to be investing the assignment with value for the student, and demonstrating that the instructor values it as well (Fagan, 1984).

Hardy (1982) and Fagan (1984) suggested several strategies to protect against plagiarism:

1. Place limits on topic selection. It is valuable to allow students the greatest possible latitude in selection of topics, but too much latitude increases the likelihood of the use of term paper mills. At the outset of the course, provide each student with a specific list of topics, then allow each student to select a topic within that range. Be sure, however, to change these topics frequently.

2. Establish precise criteria for paper format and reject any that deviate.

3. Give specific objectives for papers, and establish precise criteria for grading.

4. Have students turn in a tentative bibliography on a specific date early in the term indicating the location of all relevant sources in the library.

5. Require students to hand in an outline of their term paper before they proceed to write it.

6. Do not allow students to change their topics late in the semester. Procrastinators are particularly prone to plagiarism.

7. Give a pop test a few days before the papers are due to test basic knowledge that will appear in them.

8. Do not permit photocopied papers, accept only originally typed manuscripts.

9. Insist that students turn in all their notes and rough drafts in a file with the paper.

10. Keep all papers on file for at least five years. If students want copies of their paper, tell them to photocopy them before they turn them in for a grade.

Computers

The misuse of computers is an ever growing concern of academic institutions. Often this misuse may be considered academic dishonesty. For instance, students may turn in another student's program as their own. With the high utilization of word processing, students may be turning in papers and projects done by other students. In these cases, the instructor needs to be sure that the work turned in matches the student's abilities.

The authors were unable to find any research on academic dishonesty related to computers. In addition, faculty who teach computer courses are often reluctant to disclose the methods they use to detect cheating. They fear that students would use this information to devise ways to "beat the system."

While faculty may be reluctant to publish their methods, they should discuss the problem of computer dishonesty among themselves and share with each other their systems to combat academic dishonesty. There are several ways to prevent cheating in courses where computers are used extensively.

One of the most obvious techniques that can be employed to keep others from illegally accessing a program or data is to keep both the program and/or data on removable media such as floppy discs, which, when not in use can be stored on-site in locked media cabinets or with proper care, remain in the possession of the instructor.

Where storage of programs and data within the computer's "on board" memory is more desirable, practically all mainframe or multiuser systems provide for the use of access codes or "passwords" that can limit access to the computer itself, to only portions of the directory of programs and data files stored in memory or to the specific program providing access to data, such as test questions, etc. The frequent changing of passwords would provide effective security against all but the most determined intruder.

Encryptographic programs are also available that provide another barrier to illegal access to information by "scrambling" the data file so that it is unreadable. Then, only the proper use of the same encrypting program (which can remain always in the user's possession on a floppy disc) will restore the directory to readable form. Where the added security of such programs is desirable, their cost is modest and they are most effectively obtained through the company that has provided or services your computer system.

For ordinary classes, however, the best prevention strategy is similar to that employed in other classes—developing precise predetermined objectives. For example, in courses requiring repetitive work, where in-class assignments are completed on micros, the computer can keep accurate track of errors and error rates. No matter how much assistance has been received out of class, a student's progress will be recorded during the in-class exercises.

Where assignments call for understanding concepts rather than repetitive work, predetermined objectives become even more important. For example, in management courses which require students to be able to generate and analyze data, they can develop their own spread sheets which can then be used for test purposes. Each application is different for each student and in-class exams would require students to perform operations with unique data. In addition, students who have not done their own work out of class will not be able to complete in-class applications.

The importance of in-class applications of concepts and taking the time to develop precise predetermined objectives can not be overemphasized.

Finally, as in other areas, the course syllabus must specify what types of collaboration are and are not permitted on assignments. Academic dishonesty using computers is similar to other forms of academic dishonesty—you do not leave scoring keys lying around and neither should you make passwords accessible, you should change test items frequently and you need to do the same thing with passwords. You need to specify how students can and can not collaborate in regular courses and also in those that use computers. You need to provide opportunities for in-class exercises for traditional courses and similar procedures need to be employed in classes that utilize computers. Academic dishonesty can be prevented in courses that use computers but it takes an awareness of the problem and the time to create predetermined objectives that are precise and measurable.

SUMMARY TABLE

Table 2 provides a brief, easy-to-follow chart of all the prevention strategies presented in this chapter.

TABLE II. — SUMMARY OF PREVENTION STRATEGIES FOR ACADEMIC DISHONESTY

Types of Cheating	Detection	Prevention Strategies
1. ALL TYPES OF CHEATING	• Constant attention to details of prevention strategies. • Student help.	• Stress students' ethical and moral responsibilities to avoid cheating and to help prevent others from cheating. • Clarify policies regarding cheating and penalties for those who do cheat. • Set up a "hotline" where students can anonymously report incidents of cheating. • Individually counsel with students caught cheating or suspected of cheating—may prevent future cheating.
2. TEST PREPARATION **Obtaining a copy of the test**	• Student's responses seem beyond abilities. • Pattern of wrong answers by students known to associate with each other.	• Test should be secured in safe place by instructor from formation to administration • When word processing is used in test preparation, avoid leaving the information on the computer. If possible, place the information on a disc which can be secured in a safe place. • Tests should be original, not repetitions of exams given previous semesters.

3. TEST TAKING	• Carefully proctor exams.	• Instructors should walk around the room.
		• When giving multiple choice or short answer tests, alternate test forms should be used. A computer can be used to scramble questions and create an answer key for each different test.
a. Copying		• Spread out students using randomized seating so that every other column of seats is empty.
b. Crib sheets and other means of having answers in classroom		• All books, papers, and personal belongings should be stored under the student's seat or, preferably, in the front of the classroom.
		• Paper should be provided for the test answers and any scratch work. Staple together answer sheets and scratch paper prior to distribution with answer sheet on bottom. do not permit papers to be unstapled.
		• If blue books are to be used, require students to turn them in blank at the class period prior to the test. The books can be distributed at the start of the test.
c. Passing answers		• Give essay exams rather than True/False and multiple choice tests.
		• Do not permit any communication between students.
		• Test pick-up—have students leave their test package on their desks. This will prevent switching papers and will allow detection of copying from neighbors by answer patterns.

Types of Cheating	Detection	Prevention Strategies
d. "Ringer" taking the test for another student	• Carefully proctor exams. • Check student ID's.	• Have each student display their photo ID on the desk. Proctor can go around to check for substitutions. • Have each student hand in the test personally and present his/her ID. The instructor, having inspected the ID, checks the class roster, the name on the test, and initials the test.
"Stooge" who sits in on exam and leaves with test	• Be vigilant—try to have a proctor watch each exit. • Check ID's early.	• Number all tests before distribution. Be sure all tests are returned. If one is missing, be sure it does not show up later. • If a student needs to leave the room during a test, have him/her hand in the exam until he/she returns.
4. FOLLOWING THE TEST a. Turning in lifted exam as test taken in class	• Close observation.	• Do not leave exams or grade book on the desk or in the open unattended. Keep in locked safe place. • If a test is discovered missing at end of exam, be sure it does not reappear as completed test.
b. Changing grades on exams c. Changing answers on exams	• Photocopy the tests of those suspected before handing them back.	• Mark grades in grade book prior to returning tests. • Warn students that some exams will be photocopied before returning to detect changes. • If grades are placed on a computer, insure security is of the highest level. Place grades on disc, if possible, so that the disc can be safely locked up.

5. TAKE-HOME TEST **Take-home test done by "expert"**	• Solution done in a way not covered by instructor. • Looks "professional."	• Avoid giving take-home tests. • Require oral presentation.
6. HOMEWORK / REPORTS **a. Copy solutions from instructor's manual**	• Compare solutions with manual.	• Change to a book with no manual.
b. Copy solutions from fellow students **c. Copy from old sets from previous semesters**	• Careful grading—look for similarities.	• Count homework as only a small percentage of final grade or not at all. • Give different homework assignments each semester.
d. Get report done by expert	• Solutions done in a way not covered by instructor.	• Ask for oral presentation.

Types of Cheating	Detection	Prevention Strategies
7. PLAGIARISM	• Look for significant fluctuations in writing style. • Looks "professional." • Look for work that appears to be clearly beyond student's ability. • Compare with in-class writing assignments.	• Place limits on topic selection. • Avoid topics that are "too general"—decreases likelihood of using a "paper mill." • Change topic lists frequently. • Establish precise format for paper and stick to it. • Require a tentative bibliography early in the term. Require library location numbers. • Require advance outline of paper. • Do not permit late topic changes. • Give pop test on basic knowledge. • Accept only originally typed manuscripts—no photocopies. • Require notes and rough drafts. • Keep original papers on file for five years. • Use in class writing assignments.

NOTE: Adapted from Singhal, A.C. & Johnson, P. (1983). How to halt student dishonesty. *College Student Journal*, 17(1), 13-19. Copyright by Project Innovation. Reprinted by permission.

CONCLUSION

The evidence suggests that few if any courses or instructors are immune from acts of academic dishonesty. Instructors should no longer be considered "paranoid" for assuming that cheating can occur in their classrooms. Given enough pressure under the right conditions, almost any student might resort to dishonest behavior. The purpose of this publication is to alert readers to some of those pressures and conditions that facilitate or even encourage academic dishonesty. The purpose of this chapter has been to offer some important tips to detect and prevent academic dishonesty in the future. It is hoped that these suggestions may help enable students to be evaluated henceforth solely on the basis of merit in a fair and equitable manner.

Prevention of academic dishonesty is similar to risk management in that the possibilities become overwhelming if one spends too much time worrying about it. To take every necessary precaution to insure that no cheating ever occurs would probably leave little time for anything else. Our responsibility is to do what we can to minimize the opportunities. The strategies presented here, adapted to individual teaching and testing styles, can help to accomplish that goal.

Chapter IV

The Law and Academic Integrity

Gary Pavela

INTRODUCTION

There will be legal issues which must be considered in developing a comprehensive program to protect academic integrity on campus. First, it will be necessary to determine if academic dishonesty is to be considered a disciplinary offense, or a matter of academic judgment. Second, clear and equitable standards and procedures for resolving academic dishonesty cases will need to be developed. Third, faculty members and others responsible for reporting or resolving allegations of academic dishonesty must be advised of pertinent legal risks, including the law of defamation. Finally, considerable thought must be given to the nature of any penalties to be imposed. As will be outlined in the present chapter, these legal issues can be resolved with assurance that college and university faculty members acting reasonably and in good faith have little to fear in terms of legal liability.

Disciplinary Offense or Academic Judgment?

The question of whether academic dishonesty is an "academic" or "disciplinary" offense is a perennial subject of debate on campus. Those not affiliated with an institution of higher education may regard the topic as being somewhat esoteric, but it does have important legal and policy implications. Unfortunately, the issues are confused by the fact that campus jurisdictional boundaries are often involved, with offices responsible for student governance and academic affairs competing for appropriate decision-making authority.

Basically, academic dishonesty should be regarded as being an offense which is disciplinary in nature, although its control is essential to the academic enterprise, and to academic administration. A number of courts recognize such a relationship, and refer to "academic discipline" in pertinent cases (See, e.g. *Clayton*, 1985, p. 434; *Jones*, 1983, p. 715; *Napolitano*, 1982, p. 271). This means that basic due process protections should be provided when students are accused of academic dishonesty, although the nature of the due process may differ from that applied in other kinds of student discipline.

The best conceptual framework for examining the "disciplinary offense/academic judgment" issue can be found in the decision of the United States Supreme Court in *Board of Curators of the University of Missouri v. Horowitz* (1978). There, Justice (now Chief Justice) Rehnquist outlined two key distinctions between disciplinary and academic decision-making:

a. an academic evaluation "is by its nature more subjective and evaluative" than the "typical factual questions" encountered in the "average disciplinary decision;" and

b. disciplinary proceedings "automatically" bring "an adversarial flavor to the normal student-teacher relationship. The same conclusion does not follow in the academic context," (p. 90).

Allegations of academic dishonesty are premised upon past actions rather than present competency. Accordingly, the testimony of witnesses may be important (e.g. was a student observed copying answers from a classmate's examination paper?) as might certain forms of physical evidence (e.g. an apparent crib sheet). Basically, one needs to ask whether a neutral decision-maker would think it likely that relevant questioning of the parties could produce a definitive answer to some matter in dispute. If determination of a grade were the sole issue, detailed questioning of the faculty member might elicit answers which could properly be grounded upon matters of personal opinion and judgment. Since some sort of hearing in these or comparable circumstances would not merit a considerable expenditure of time and resources, the most the courts are likely to require will be a "careful and deliberate" decision (*Board of Curators*, 1978, p. 132) based upon "professional judgment" (*Regents of University of Michigan* 1985, p. 533). On the other hand, a student accused of academic dishonesty might very well be able to elicit empirical facts which could clearly and decisively affect the final decision. Providing an opportunity for some type of hearing seems appropriate in the latter circumstance, especially if some serious penalty might be imposed.

There will be hazily defined areas between academic judgments and disciplinary determinations, partly due to the fact that both forms of decision-making inevitably combine elements of subjective and objective analysis. For example, resolving a charge of plagiarism when no original source has been discovered is a subtle task, and may depend upon impressionistic comparisons of a current piece of writing with prior efforts. Nonetheless, given the fact that faculty members are generally reluctant to pursue such allegations, it seems unreasonable to mold the entire process of resolving all academic dishonesty cases to fit the most extreme and rare exceptions to the norm. A better solution would be to insure faculty participation on the panels or hearing boards created to resolve such matters.

The second component of Justice Rehnquist's test is even more dispositive. If one had to receive an "F" in a course, most individuals would feel that harm would be compounded by an accompanying finding of academic dishonesty. While a single failing grade may be attributed to a wide variety of understandable circumstances, failure attributed to academic fraud is another matter; it reflects upon the recipient's character, and has the potential to produce a lasting stigma. This is precisely the circumstance which brings an "adversarial flavor" to most disciplinary cases. The adversarial element is a natural by-product of a process designed, in part, to be an effective deterrent.

Many educators would agree with an observation in a 1979 Carnegie Council Report that "penalties for willful dishonesty must be severe because truth is the stock and trade of the academic community," (*Fair Practices*, p. 58.). Yet the need to impose severe penalties presents a genuine dilemma for those who would regard academic dishonesty as a purely academic matter. Essentially, the threat of a stigmatizing penalty is the most compelling deterrent available in an educational community. Students see such penalties as being severe because they are fearful that a history of dishonesty, made a part of their educational records, will reflect adversely upon their character, thereby reducing the career opportunities available to them. However, when stigmatizing penalties are imposed, courts are much more likely to regard the entire process as being disciplinary in nature, if not in name. See *Anderson*, 1972 (student accused of examination tampering subject to "disciplinary proceeding" and entitled to a hearing with "a full opportunity to present his defenses," p. 536); *Goldberg*, 1967 (Conduct such as "cheating on an examination" may be "disciplined by the University," p. 476); *Hall*, 1984 ("cheating" as "disciplinary" offense, p. 308); *Henson*, 1983 (Student accused of violating honor code by removing moot court problem was subject to "disciplinary" proceeding, p. 74); *Jaska*, 1984 ("cheating should be treated as a disciplinary matter" and "requires greater procedural protection than academic dismissals" since "dismissal for cheating" is "more stigmatizing," p. 1248, N. 2); *Lightsey*, 1983 (cheating case "a disciplinary matter rather than an academic one . . . despite the artful semantics" of campus officials, p. 648); *Mary M.*, 1984 (student accused of cheating was involved in "disciplinary proceedings" and was entitled to the "due process requirements" commonly associated with disciplinary cases, pp. 844-845); *McDonald*, 1974 (student in cheating case "disciplined" for "offense . . . unique to the academic community" and entitled to "full and fair hearing" before expulsion, p. 104); *Nash*, 1985 (veterinary students accused of cheating were entitled to "procedural due process in the context of a school disciplinary proceeding," although such due process "does not require all the trappings . . . of a criminal trial," p. 953); *Slaughter*, 1975 (unauthorized use of advisor's name on publication "was one on the conduct or ethical side rather than an academic deficiency," p. 624).

Careful consideration of Justice Rehnquist's distinctions between academic and disciplinary determinations indicates that academic dishonesty should be equated with a disciplinary offense. It is for this reason that most courts have held that students subject to academic dishonesty charges should be entitled to some basic due process protections. Even the small number of cases in which academic dishonesty was regarded as a matter of "academic" judgment did not produce a different result. See *Corso*, 1984 (cheating on examination and subsequent lying about the offense are "clearly an academic matter," p. 532); *Napolitano*, 1982 (plagiarism involves "academic standards and not . . . violation of rules of conduct," p. 273). Significantly, both Creighton University in *Corso* and Princeton University in *Napolitano* already had policies which provided for basic due process protections, at least when serious penalties could be imposed. It was relatively painless for the courts to apply an "academic" label, knowing that the cases in question would be processed in accordance with the standard due process procedures associated with student discipline. Indeed, in *Corso*, the court required the university to adhere to its own policies in that regard. What was not confronted in either case was a situation in which campus regulations, properly applied, would allow a student to be suspended or expelled for academic dishonesty without notice, an explanation of the evidence, and an opportunity to be heard.

Regardless of whether the "academic" or "disciplinary" label is applied, the simple fact is that both public and private colleges and universities are almost certainly going to provide students with some type of a hearing in cases involving academic dishonesty. Given the omnipresent fear of litigation, and the (generally overstated) risk of personal liability, it is not feasible to expect that faculty members would be willing to resolve such matters by themselves, especially if sanctions of suspension or expulsion may be involved. Grade penalties alone will not be sufficient, since even a grade of "F" is not an effective deterrent to a student already in danger of failing a course. Also, some mechanism is needed to identify and punish repeat offenders. These practical considerations require the creation of reporting procedures, and the involvement of campus administrators. Since administrators will rarely have personal knowledge of a reported incident, it would be foolhardy for them to accept all the legal and public relations risks associated with suspending or expelling students who have not been accorded some reasonable opportunity to respond to the charges against them. In short, if the "academic" label is still applied in these circumstances, it will be to define jurisdictional boundaries within the campus administration, rather than as a license for the unfettered exercise of faculty discretion.

Legal considerations and practical necessities are not the only reasons for according students some due process protections in academic dishonesty cases. The issue is also one of ethics, and pertains to the teaching of values. Basically, educators would be well served by a simple reliance upon the Golden Rule as a starting point for the examination of campus policies. If faculty members and administrators would expect to have some structured opportunity to defend themselves before being subject to a serious penalty for an alleged act of fraud, they should be bound as a matter of logic and conscience to accord similar protections to students. In doing so, they are not only teaching the value of reciprocity, but affirming Justice Jackson's admonition that "due process of law is not for the sole benefit of the accused . . . (i)t is the best insurance against those blunders which leave lasting stains on a system of justice," and which are "bound to occur" when individuals are given unchecked authority (*Shaughnessy*, 1953, pp. 224-225).

Furthermore, the power of moral condemnation associated with disciplinary language and disciplinary procedures compels students to view their misbehavior from an ethical perspective. The normal excuses for inadequate academic performance are simply not relevant in a context where the focus of inquiry is upon the principle of right and wrong (e.g. gaining an unfair advantage over others by cheating). Properly designed disciplinary proceedings can constitute a form of morality play, in which all the participants define and endorse a number of important virtues. Educators should not seek to evade this occasionally frustrating but genuinely important process on the grounds of administrative convenience, or campus politics.

Regardless of the arguments which might be presented, it is inevitable that some educators will remain tempted to misapply the academic label in certain disciplinary cases. Those who do so run a substantial risk of becoming victims of their own handiwork. See *Brookins*, 1973 (student dismissed on what nursing school called "academic" grounds was entitled to a "due process hearing," since his failure to report prior enrollment elsewhere, along with other offenses, involved "disputed facts" concerning compliance "with certain school regulations." pp. 382-383); *Regents of University of Michigan* 1985, p. 532 (although refusal to allow student to retake the examination was a "genuinely" academic decision, different result could be reached if campus officials are found to be "concealing nonacademic or constitutionally impermissible reasons" for dismissal); *Lightsey* 1983 (refusal to rescind failing grade for cheating after student was exonerated by hearing panel was "arbitrary and capricious," raises questions about

the institution's "good faith," and was not a matter of "academic standards," pp. 650, 648); *Sofair*, 1978 ("judicial evidentiary hearing" might
have been required for public university student if "assignment of
academic cause" had been "a calculated pretext" for his dismissal, p.
731); *Woody*, 1966 (student considered to be a "disturbing influence
in classes" was improperly denied permission to register "because the
faculty committee, instead of bringing open charges of misconduct
in the usual manner before the disciplinary committee . . . abrogated
unto itself the authority of imposing its own penalty . . ." (pp. 57-59).

Ongoing debate and confusion concerning the application of
"academic" or "disciplinary" labels could be minimized if college and
university officials understand that academic dishonesty is both
academic and disciplinary in nature. Since honesty is vital to the
academic enterprise, it is reasonable to accord faculty members and
academic administrators a substantial role in resolving academic
dishonesty cases. However, use of the academic label in such cases
is primarily useful for defining jurisdictional responsibilities; it should
not be misapplied to deny rudimentary due process to students who
are subject to serious, stigmatizing penalties for actions which constitute a violation of campus regulations. Ideally, traditional administrative boundaries on campus can be crossed by creating procedures which can accommodate the compelling interests of academic
decision-makers, while drawing upon the experience and expertise of
campus officials who regularly resolve other types of disciplinary cases.
Finally, as will be set forth below, there are sound policy reasons for
involving student leaders and student organizations in determining
academic integrity policies, and in resolving individual cases.

DUE PROCESS PROCEDURES

Complex, trial-type procedures need not be followed in academic
dishonesty cases, or in other cases involving student discipline. Nonetheless, at many campuses across the country, disciplinary systems
have become "mired in legalistic disputes over rules or evidence" (Lamont, 1979, p. 85). As a result, students are encouraged to view campus disciplinary hearings as an "intricate chess game of procedural
moves and countermoves" (American Council on Education, 1983, p.
15), rather than a means to ascertain pertinent facts and to produce
a just outcome. The attitudes which are fostered by such a process
are particularly pernicious in academic dishonesty cases, since faculty
members are understandably reluctant to pursue allegations in what
may appear to be the functional equivalent of a criminal trial. As a
consequence, some faculty members ignore academic dishonesty alto-
gether, thereby putting honest students at a competitive disadvantage.
Others simply lower the grades of students whom they presume

guilty of cheating or plagiarism. Both practices injure students without any due process at all, and prevent identification of repeat offenders.

Educators at both public and private institutions will want to assure students basic procedural fairness in resolving disciplinary allegations. Such a practice would be a requirement of constitutional law at a public college or university (*Dixon*, 1961), an explicit or implied term of the contract of enrollment at a private school (*Slaughter*, 1975), and an exercise in common sense and decency in any event. Due process, however, is not an end in itself; a careful balance must be struck between procedural protection, and other important community interests, including the maintenance of reasonable standards of civility and integrity.

A first step in developing appropriate due process procedures is to understand that "due process is flexible and calls for such procedural protections as the particular situation demands" (Morrissey, 1972, p. 481). For example, if a range of possible penalties can be determined in advance, students who are subject to lesser penalties need not be accorded as much due process as students who could be suspended or expelled. Indeed, a student who could only be given a reprimand, or assigned to a brief community service project, would simply be entitled to "oral or written notice of the charges against him and, if he denies them, an explanation of the evidence the authorities have and an opportunity to present his side of the story" in an informal "discussion" with a school official (*Goss*, 1975, pp. 581-582). The rationale for this common sense approach was best expressed by a federal judge in Kentucky, who observed that if educators have to make "a federal case out of every petty disciplinary incident, the whole purpose of having any discipline at all and any rules of conduct would be defeated" (*Bahr*, 1982, p. 487).

It will also be important to understand that students who are subject to stricter sanctions (and, accordingly, to more due process protection) may request to have their cases resolved informally. If the institution grants such a request, the student's decision can be binding, if freely and knowingly made, even though suspension, expulsion or the imposition of a stigmatizing penalty might result. (*Yench*, 1973, *North*, 1985). However, care should be taken to insure that students are informed in writing of all the risks associated with any waiver of due process rights and are provided a reasonable amount of time to consider their decision and to confer with a family member or advisor.

Even if some sort of hearing must be held in an academic dishonesty case, it will not be necessary to conduct a full-fledged adversarial proceeding. For example, in *Mary M.* (1984) a New York State appellate court reiterated that:

[p]etitioner was served with a written notice of charges; she was made aware of grounds which would justify her expulsion or suspension by way of the student handbook; the hearing tribunal afforded her an opportunity to hear and confront the evidence presented against her and an opportunity to be heard and to offer other evidence if she chose; she was accorded the right to have someone from the college community to assist her in the proceedings; she was informed of the tribunal's finding; she was given access to its decision for her personal review; and, finally, she was advised in writing of the discipline imposed. We find that this procedure adequately satisfied due process requirements in a collegial atmosphere (p. 4).

The *Mary M.* case, and holdings such as *Dixon* (1961), *Esteban* (1967), a Missouri federal court "General Order" (1968), *Morale* (1976), *Sohmer* (1982), *Jaska* (1984) and *Nash* (1985), all indicate that courts have given educational institutions considerable flexibility in designing equitable and efficient due process procedures. Such flexibility is desirable because it permits reasonable experimentation in developing different methods of resolving disputes (*University of Houston*, 1984, p. 689). Indeed, given the constructive criticism directed toward the larger legal system (See, e.g. Bok, 1983), and the absence of imaginative procedural thinking in law schools or the legal profession as a whole, (Davis, 1971, p. 228), thoughtful innovations developed in campus communities may have broad application elsewhere. Colleges and universities offer leadership in a wide range of areas—in science and technology, for example—across the entire spectrum of social needs. There is no reason why that leadership should not extend to alternative methods of adjudication and conflict resolution. Student affairs administrators in particular have many opportunities in this regard. Unfortunately, those opportunities have largely been wasted, due to an uncritical and ritualistic adherence to the traditional adversary system.

One innovation which has developed and can be expanded upon at campuses across the country has been a reliance upon investigatory hearing procedures. Essentially, instead of depending upon a passive jury to consider the conflicting arguments presented by opposing counsel, the investigatory model would permit members of the hearing panel to examine the case file beforehand, and question witnesses at the hearing. Such a system gives much more active control of the proceeding to the decision-maker. Properly used, it also protects the legitimate interests of the accused student, since complainants would be subject to thorough questioning by hearing panel members. The courts are familiar with this approach in other administrative proceedings, and certainly can be persuaded that it is not inappropriate in student disciplinary cases. See, e.g. *Clayton*, 1975: combination of "prosecutorial and judicial functions" does not necessarily preclude "a fair and impartial fact-finding process," p. 425; see also, *Crook*, 1987; Friendly, 1975; Frankel, 1975; Burger, 1984.

An important advantage of the investigatory model is a limitation upon the role of counsel. The courts are virtually unanimous in holding that the full and active participation of lawyers is not a requirement of due process in student disciplinary cases at institutions of higher education. See *Crook*, 1987, *Nash* (1985, pp. 957-958 and extensive citations therein), *Jaska* (1984), *Mary M.* (1984), and *University of Houston* (1984). Most judges are experienced lawyers, and fully appreciate that the formalism often associated with aggressive legal representation can do more harm than good to accused students in an educational setting (See *Jackson*, 1970, p. 217; ". . . an adversary atmosphere . . . would hardly best serve the interests of any of those involved.;" *Mary M.*, 1984, p. 845: ". . . the student's welfare is best served by a nonadversarial setting;" Bok, D., p. 42, 1983: ". . . complicating the rules and insisting on an adversary process . . . can undermine justice in many types of cases."). This perspective has been shared by experienced educators across the country, who "have observed some incredible courtroom tactics" used by lawyers in campus disciplinary proceedings "which have prolonged the process, irritated the judicial body, and no doubt influenced the final judgment, perhaps negatively" (Steele, Johnson, Rickard, 1983, p. 15).

Many of the attorneys who represent students in disciplinary cases lack interest or experience in informal nonadversarial proceedings. Instead, in the words of one law professor:

> Throughout their three years in law school, students are constantly reminded that the adversary process provides the foundation for our legal system. They learn that attorneys are obliged to represent their clients zealously, and they frequently conclude that appropriate representation consists of unnecessarily aggressive and litigious tactics. By the end of their third year of law school, many graduating seniors evidence frighteningly cynical perspectives regarding the legal profession. They seem to think that most practitioners will engage in dishonesty to advance the interests of their clients, and will utilize other equally dishonorable tactics whenever advantageous. I sometimes fear that too many new attorneys commence practice with the notion that they must "do unto others before they do unto them." (Craver, 1983, p. 4)

Other knowledgeable observers, including a fellow of the American College of Trial Lawyers, see a pattern of "rising aggressiveness, incivility, and cutthroat competition" in the legal profession (Brown, 1983, p. A31; see also Burger, 1987). Such competition may have ended any tradition of the lawmaker as peacemaker. "It used to be that settlement of a dispute was the first road a lawyer would take" observed a former chair of the American Bar Association Committee on Delivery of Legal Services, "now settlement is the last road we take" (Huckaby, 1983, p. 8).

Lawyers commonly cultivate an aura of unrelenting self assurance, partly as a means to attract and retain clients, and because they assume that the rhetorical skills honed in the courtroom are readily applicable in other settings. Consequently, when representing an individual who is young and inexperienced, lawyers may be tempted to engage in protracted argumentation about "Miranda" warnings and other procedural rules which have not been applied in the college and university environment. These tactics may satisfy the client's immediate desire for a "vigorous" defense, and gratify the lawyer's ego; unfortunately, they also create a dangerously negative image of the accused student, who may have paid a substantial fee for such a "service."

It is sometimes suggested that the harm which attorneys may occasionally inflict upon their own clients in an educational setting could be minimized if more effective leadership were exercised by those who preside at disciplinary proceedings. What is often overlooked, however, is that faculty members or students who conduct administrative hearings lack the authority and resources of a state or federal judge, even though they may be confronted with adversarial tactics that even the courts have difficulty in managing (see, e.g. Burger, 1984; Martineau, 1984). One prominent defense attorney's description of the typical criminal courtroom provides a chilling insight into the atmosphere which educators are rightly determined to avoid:

> Judge, prosecutor, and defense lawyers are caught up together in the elaborate network of interminable adversary procedures for presenting evidence. Everyone is horribly afraid of making a blunder. Contentiousness and deviousness are heavy in the air, and malice and rancor flash out from time to time. (Hughes, 1982, p. 27)

Within broad ethical limits[1] lawyers are trained to rely upon the arts of deception in what is presumed to be a balanced adversarial contest (see Strick, 1977; Dershowitz, 1982). Judge Friendly has observed, for example, "causing delay and sowing confusion not only are [the lawyer's] right but may be his duty" (Friendly, 1975, p. 1288; See also Justice Harlan's dissent in *Miranda*, 1966, p. 514: "the lawyer in fulfilling his professional responsibilities of necessity may become an obstacle to truthfinding"). Transposing this system into the college and university environment, without benefit of the necessary checks and controls available in the courts, invites counsel for accused students to attempt to dominate the entire fact finding process. Some are successful in doing so, and may prevent an occasional injustice from being done. Others generate a hostile reaction from hearing panel

---

[1]Ethical limits for lawyers are sometimes hard to discern. See comments of Stephen Gillers, Professor of Evidence and Ethics at the New York University Law School: "Not only is it not unethical to try to cast aspersions on the character of the victim, it's ethically the lawyer's duty to do that if it will succeed in a not-guilty verdict . . ." (cited in Freedman, 1986, p. 1).

members who work in an environment in which collegiality and the rigorous pursuit of truth are cherished ideals.

Essentially, lawyers tend to view justice as a process rather than a particular result (Dershowitz, 1982, p. 416). Most educators, however, are concerned with student moral development, and are frustrated when lawyers appear to transform ethical questions into procedural issues. Both lawyers and educators have reasonable perspectives. Given enough time, and a willingness to engage in dialogue, they could even reach some conceptual understanding. However, in most contested cases, students will be caught in the middle between radically different perspectives. Under these circumstances, while it may be prudent to seek the advice of counsel in serious cases, most students will be far better off speaking for themselves in internal campus proceedings.

Partly as a result of a limitation upon the role of counsel for any party, the investigatory model for due process hearings also has the advantage of promoting discussion and dialogue between the accused student and the hearing panel. Such personal interaction is designed to create a different atmosphere from that often encountered in the criminal courts, where "outcomes do not seem to be determined by principles or careful consideration of persons, but by hustling, conning, manipulating, bargaining, luck, fortitude, waiting them out, and the like" (Casper, 1972, p. 18). An important educational objective in encouraging dialogue is to "express the elementary idea that to be a *person*, rather than a *thing*, is at least to be *consulted* about what is done with one." (Tribe, 1978, p. 503). Furthermore, there is always the very real possibility that candid discussion of the issues may permit examination of pertinent regulations, and facilitate subsequent improvement in campus policies (Kirp, 1976).

If candid discussion and dialogue are desirable components of the investigatory hearing process, those who design campus disciplinary policies will want to avoid any misapplication of the Fifth Amendment right to remain silent, or of the Fourth Amendment "exclusionary rule." Essentially, the Fifth Amendment is designed to prevent self-incrimination in *criminal* cases, and may not be invoked unless there is a possibility of criminal prosecution. Even if the student could be subject to some concurrent criminal charge (e.g. forgery of a transcript), it would be prudent for the institution to have a policy of drawing an "adverse inference" (as opposed to an automatic finding of guilt) from a student's refusal to speak. Ironically, this seemingly harsh policy may protect students "placed between the rock and the whirlpool," since there is viable case law holding that testimony elicited in such circumstances could not be used in subsequent criminal proceedings (*Garrity*, 1967; *Nzuve*, 1975; *Furutani*, 1969; *Goldberg*, 1967).

Likewise, individuals accused of academic dishonesty may occasionally contend that critical evidence (e.g., a crib sheet) was "illegally" seized, and may not be considered as evidence in a subsequent hearing. Educators, however, do have broader authority than law enforcement officers in seizing contraband or conducting searches (*Moore*, 1968; *New Jersey*, 1985). Moreover, unlike the Fifth Amendment, the exclusionary rule is a judge-made provision, not mentioned in the Constitution, which has been subject to substantial modification over the years (see Pavela, 1983, pp. 25-26). Given other legal protections available to students as a means to deter official misconduct (see, e.g. Wood, 1975), the exclusionary rule would be an unnecessary obstacle to examination and discussion of relevant evidence in an educational setting. (See *Morale*, 1976, p. 1001: the "Supreme Court clearly intends to limit the exclusionary rule . . . and to allow only a criminal defendant to invoke its protections.")

There are a myriad of other procedural questions that can be raised in academic dishonesty hearings. Generally, as outlined below, the courts have required little more than what common sense would dictate as standards of fairness:

1. Students subject to serious sanctions are entitled to a written statement of the specific charges against them. Also, before any hearing or conference, students should be allowed to examine any written evidence or exhibits which the institution plans to submit (*Esteban*, 1967).

2. Students who are entitled to a hearing should be informed of the hearing date, time, and location, and should be given reasonable time to prepare a defense. One court has suggested that ten days notice would be sufficient (*Speake*, 1970). Also, absent a showing of prejudice, more than one charge against a student can be considered at a hearing (*Turof*, 1981).

3. A hearing may be conducted in the absence of a student who fails to appear after campus officials have made a reasonable effort to provide adequate advance notice of the hearing time, date, and location (*Wright*, 1968).

4. The Family Education Rights and Privacy Act (20 U.S.C. 1232(g)) would preclude holding an "open" hearing without the consent of the accused student (*correspondence to the author from the Department of Education*, November 20, 1981). It might be sound policy to permit an open hearing if the student so requests, but at least one court has indicated that there is no constitutional right to an open disciplinary hearing in the educational setting (*Hart*, 1983).

5. Hearings need not be delayed until after a student has been tried on any concurrent criminal charges (*Goldberg*, 1967; *Nzuve*, 1975; *Hart*, 1983).

6. A reasonable effort should be made to accommodate the schedule of any advisor allowed to assist the accused student. For example, if campus rules permit a legal advisor, an attorney who affirms that he or she must appear in court at the same time as a disciplinary hearing should be given a continuance. Nonetheless, hearing officers retain broad discretion in granting continuances, and need not permit attorneys or others to delay disciplinary proceedings without compelling justification (see *Morris*, 1983). An important consideration in determining whether attorneys will be allowed to participate in academic dishonesty hearings is the risk that professional counsel may be very skillful in turning a relatively simple proceeding into a protracted case. For example, writing in 1985, the West Virginia Supreme Court observed in *North:*

> Although we have disparaged Mr. North's arguments, we have nothing but surpassing admiration for Mr. North's counsel, Mr. Edgar F. Heiskell, who has doggedly, diligently, and skillfully kept Mr. North's case alive since 1977. In fact, Mr. Heiskell, at points, almost accomplished a miracle. But finally, and given the amount of money the State of West Virginia has spent on Mr. North's education, reluctantly, we must affirm the circuit court, which did an equally thorough job in reviewing this case. (1985, p. 147)

7. None of the cases setting forth general due process requirements has indicated that students must be appointed to serve on disciplinary hearing panels, although "having an administrator as the 'sole judge' in serious cases may be 'undesirable' on policy grounds" (*Winnick*, 1972, p. 548). Establishment of a racial quota for membership on judicial panels at public institutions might be unconstitutional (*Uzzell*, 1984).

8. Individuals serving on disciplinary hearing panels need not be disqualified because they have a superficial knowledge of the background of the case, or because they may know the participants. The basic test is whether or not the panelists can "judge the case fairly and solely on the evidence presented . . ." (*Keene*, 1970, p. 222; see also, *Wasson*, 1967, *Jones*, 1968, *Winnick*, 1972; and *Blanton*, 1973). However, hearing panelists should not have participated in investigating or prosecuting the case (*Marshall*, 1980). A very recent case, currently being appealed, also suggests that administrative officers involved in ruling on procedural issues prior to a hearing may compromise a hearing board's independence if they participate in subsequent board deliberations, even as a non-voting member (*Gorman*, 1986, p. 811).

9. The "beyond a reasonable doubt" standard of proof used in criminal cases need not be adopted in campus disciplinary proceedings. Instead, at least one court has held that a student's guilt should be established by "clear and convincing evidence" (*Smyth*, 1975, p. 799; Long, 1985).

10. Circumstantial evidence may be used in criminal proceedings and campus disciplinary cases (*McDonald*, 1974). Likewise, colleges are not required to exclude "hearsay" evidence, although it would be unwise to base a finding of guilt on hearsay evidence alone. Most other technical rules of evidence are not applicable in campus disciplinary proceedings (*Goldberg*, 1967; *Henson*, 1983; *Mary M.* 1984).

11. Cases need not be dismissed on the ground that school officials failed to give students "Miranda" warnings about the right to remain silent. The Miranda rule has not been extended to the educational setting (*Boynton*, 1982).

12. A student subject to a serious penalty should be permitted to confront and cross-examine witnesses if the case will be decided on questions of credibility (*Winnick*, 1972; but see *Nash*, 1985). However, the institution is not required to devise a means to compel the attendance of witnesses (*Turof*, 1981), although it might be a good policy to do so.

13. Hearings in serious disciplinary cases should be tape recorded or transcribed. Furthermore, students who are found guilty of the charges against them should be given written reasons for such a determination (*Morale*, 1976; *Gorman*, 1986).

14 Due process does not require that the decision of the hearing panel be unanimous. A simple majority vote would be sufficient (*Nzuve*, 1975).

15 A student who is found guilty of the charges should not be subject to an additional punishment simply for having pled innocent. However, a hearing panel may consider a pattern of lying and fabrication by the student at a hearing and may impose a more severe penalty as a result (*United States*, 1978). Likewise, a student who is found guilty of the charges and who refuses to identify other participants in the misbehavior could be subject to added punishment (*Roberts*, 1980).

16. In the absence of some sort of arbitrary discrimination, a decision to impose differing punishments in similar cases will be upheld if "reasonably and fairly made" (*Jones*, 1968, p. 203; *Napolitano*, 1982). Likewise, as in the larger society, it is not necessary to apprehend every wrongdoer before prosecuting those who have been caught (*Zanders*, 1968).

17. A just punishment imposed for reasons of deterrence is not incompatible with the educational mission of a school or college (*Petrey*, 1981; *Napolitano*, 1982).

18. Colleges and universities may establish disciplinary panels which make recommendations to an administrative officer who would review the record and the findings before making a final deter-

mination. Such a procedure may permit the administrative officer to correct any prior procedural errors (*Blanton*, 1973). Due process, however, does not require a formal right of appeal (*Reetz*, 1903; *National Union of Marine Cooks*, 1954; *Winnick*, 1972; *Nash*, 1985; Kaplin, 1978, p. 241).

19. Finally, the courts will expect both state and private institutions to follow their own regulations (*Tedeschi*, 1980; *Clayton*, 1981; *Jones*, 1983). Occasional harmless errors may be permitted, but campus officials will have to show that the deviations did not deny students a fair hearing (*Winnick*, 1972; *Turof*, 1981). Students may, of course, knowingly and freely waive a campus procedural requirement (*Yench*, 1973).

Liability for Reporting Allegations of Academic Dishonesty

One of the most common reasons given by faculty members for a reluctance to report allegations of academic dishonesty is the fear of personal liability. Even one phone call from one lawyer threatening a lawsuit in an academic dishonesty case has the potential to spawn oral accounts and histories among the faculty which would rival those of the Navajo Indian Nation. However, a careful review of the caselaw indicates that these concerns are groundless. Faculty members and others who report pertinent allegations in good faith, and in accordance with reasonable campus regulations, are amply protected by the law. There is not one reported case viable as precedent in the entire history of the Republic which indicates otherwise.

Many individuals misconceive the law as being a series of ritualistic incantations, known only to lawyers and judges, leading to some inexorable result, regardless of the social policy considerations. Nothing could be further from the truth. The essence of legal decision-making is the careful balancing of individual and community interests. In many cases, judges are doing nothing more or less than engaging in the practice of applied ethics, based upon prevalent social, moral, and economic perspectives. In most tort and constitutional law litigation, this means there is little risk of liability if educators can demonstrate that their actions were rationally related to what is perceived to be some socially useful objective, and that they treated others with common standards of fairness.

It is reasonable, of course, to be concerned about the stress and expense of a lawsuit, even if the end result is likely to be favorable. Many observers agree that our legal system could stand considerable improvement in this regard, and there is some movement toward reforms[2] which would discourage frivolous litigation. See *Meyer*, 1986,

---

[2]Modern reforms sometimes have ancient correlates. Compare Neff and Nagel, 1974, (Plaintiffs in early Greece who received less than a fifth of juror's votes were "subject to a lashing or a monetary penalty" p. 138) with Neely, 1983:
one simple change would do more than anything else to encourage dispute set-

(professor who brought "frivolous civil rights and defamation suit against University of Washington and his departmental colleagues was required to pay $50,000 in attorney fees, p. 104); *Rivera Carbana*, 1984, p. 84 (student seeking readmission and challenging course grades was a "persistent litigator" of "clearly frivolous" claims and was obligated to pay defendant's attorney's fees); *National Law Journal*, December 8, 1986, p. 3 ("In a harsh and expensive blow to a New York lawyer . . ., the 2d U.S. Circuit Court of Appeals has declared his lawsuit frivolous and affirmed an award of $555,000 in attorney fees to the defendants" p. 3, reporting *Zissu*, 1986); see, generally Martineau, 1984 ("In the past several years . . . courts have relied increasingly upon the authority granted to them by two statutes and a federal rule of appellate procedure to impose sanctions upon parties or attorneys taking frivolous appeals or using abusive tactics . . ." p. 847). College and university attorneys will want to follow these trends carefully, and to invoke available remedies in appropriate cases.[3]

When lawsuits are filed against college and university employees, most public and private institutions do provide for legal representation and indemnification, provided that the acts in question were not grossly negligent or criminal in nature, and were within the scope of employment. Details about such protection can be obtained from appropriate campus officials. Various forms of insurance are also available, although the value of such insurance for faculty members and administrators (other than physicians, therapists, or other high-risk professions) is almost certain to be largely psychological.

One fear occasionally expressed by faculty and staff members is that they may be found personally liable for violating a student's due process rights in an academic dishonesty case. Yet this risk is virtually nil, provided that reports of academic dishonesty are processed in accordance with reasonable procedures which have been fully and carefully reviewed by counsel. The United States Supreme Court has developed a strict test in this regard: educators will not be held personally responsible for violating a student's constitutional rights unless they have acted with "impermissible motivation" or with such disregard of "clearly established constitutional rights" that their "action cannot reasonably be characterized as being in good faith" (*Wood*, 1975, p. 322; See also *Picozzi*, 1986). Essentially, educators are to be given "a degree of immunity" in their work:

> however worded, the immunity must be such that public school officials understand that action taken in the good faith fulfillment

---

tlement . . . make the loser pay the other side's legal fees. Lawyers who believe their client has a good case will press ahead; those who don't will be willing to settle, or won't take the case at all, p. 44.

[3]The United States Supreme Court agreed on April 6, 1987 to consider the practice of awarding attorney fees to defendants as punishment for bringing frivolous suits. See *Washington Post* April 7, 1987, p. A6 (reference: *Haynie*, 1986).

of their responsibilities and within the bounds of reason under all the circumstances will not be punished and that they need not exercise their discretion with undue timidity. (*id*, p. 321)

Ironically, it is often those faculty members who are most fearful of litigation, and who wish to resolve academic dishonesty cases privately and "informally," who are at the greatest legal risk. For example, it may be possible for a faculty member to obtain what appears to be a student's acquiescence to an "unofficial" sanction for an apparent act of academic dishonesty. However, such acquiescence can quickly unravel (or be deemed invalid due to "coercion") when the outcome is reported to or discovered by the student's parents. The faculty member is then in the vulnerable position of having acted outside the scope of his or her authority, as defined by pertinent campus regulations, and might not be entitled to legal representation or indemnification from the institution. These or similar circumstances may have been what one federal judge had in mind when he observed in *Hill*, 1976, pp. 256-257, that "in a proper case, I could envision that a timely filed procedural due process action" against faculty members or administrators at a state institution "who personally impose a stigma-type penalty without notice and an opportunity to be heard . . . might be successful . . . ." These legal risks are compounded if faculty members or administrators insist on imposing penalties even after a student has been found "not guilty" of academic dishonesty charges by a campus hearing board authorized to make final determinations in such matters (*Lightsey*, 1983).

A second major concern for faculty members in reporting allegations of academic dishonesty at both public and private institutions is the risk of liability for defamation (i.e., in most states: oral or written falsehoods communicated to third parties which would harm a plaintiff's reputation). Concerns of this nature would be justified if faculty members discussed unsubstantiated reports of academic dishonesty with individuals not involved in investigating or processing academic dishonesty cases, or who otherwise could not be said to have a legitimate educational interest in the information (e.g., a reporter for the campus newspaper). Furthermore, even if the allegations turned out to be true, such disclosures would normally be prohibited by the Family Educational Rights and Privacy Act (34 C.F.R. Part 99) and could, in an egregious case, constitute a tortious invasion of privacy, or intentional infliction of emotional distress (e.g. public announcement of an accused student's name and the case outcome, done to humiliate and embarrass the student; see *Johnson*, 1986: disclosure of student's sexual orientation may constitute an invasion of privacy, although that cause of action was barred by statute of limitations. See, generally, Prosser, 1964, pp. 824-825).

Contrary to the previous examples, faculty members reporting allegations of academic dishonesty who adhere to basic standards of common sense and reciprocity are unlikely to be found liable for defamation, even if an allegation later turns out to be inaccurate. Again, like litigation involving constitutional rights of students, the courts consider the relevant policy issues, and accord a "privilege" to faculty members (and others) who refer allegations of wrongdoing to those who are responsible for taking appropriate action. The obvious reason for according such a privilege is to encourage the reporting and resolution of matters which are important for the protection of legitimate social interests. (See *Picozzi*, 1986, p. 1579: administrator "had a duty not to mislead other schools into thinking Picozzi was in unqualified good standing . . .")

At least one recent case has suggested that members of an academic community have an "absolute privilege" to communicate information or opinions in the course of campus proceedings which are "quasi-judicial" in nature (*Webster*, 1986, p. 34, pertaining to "tenure hearings"). An "absolute privilege" is generally interpreted to mean that the party accorded the privilege has "complete freedom of expression, without any inquiry as to . . . motives" (Prosser, 1964, p. 796), even if the facts or opinions expressed turn out to be false. Such freedom of expression would also apply to communications made as "the first step" in a quasi-judicial campus proceeding (e.g., a letter of accusation sent to an appropriate official) (*Webster*, 1986, p. 35). Another court has determined that students "impliedly" consent to "intra-school publication" of "frank evaluation(s)" by faculty members or administrative officials. Such implied consent means that appropriate evaluators are protected by an "absolute privilege" and that students have "no cause of action" for defamation, provided that the evaluations in question are relevant to a student's academic performance, and are shared only with those having "a legitimate interest in the subject matter" (*Kraft*, 1985, pp. 1149-1150).

It is by no means certain that every court would accord an absolute privilege to a referring faculty member in an academic dishonesty case. What is most likely is that the faculty member would be given a "qualified" privilege. Still, a qualified privilege is ample protection (see, *Cohen*, 1986), since it means that the faculty member's referral or report to a proper institutional official would not be actionable unless it was made in bad faith, "with knowledge it [was] false or with reckless disregard for its truth or falsity" (*Kelly*, 1985, p. 296, citing *McCarney*, 1976; see, e.g. *Melton*, 1978). The United States Supreme Court has defined "reckless disregard" to mean that a defendant must "in fact [have] entertained serious doubts as to the truth of his publication" (*St. Amant*, 1968, p. 731, cited in *Kelly, supra*). This is a difficult standard for plaintiffs to overcome, except for examples in which "a story is fabricated by the defendant, is the product of his imagination, or is based wholly on an unverified anonymous telephone call" (*St Amant*, 1968, p. 732).

Careful review of the relevant caselaw should reassure faculty members who are worried about the legal risks involved in properly reporting good faith allegations of academic dishonesty. Those who remain unconvinced may be influenced by misleading anecdotical information from their colleagues. Others will persist in citing the risk of liability in order to avoid discussion of different concerns, including a general reluctance to confront students about dishonest behavior. If the latter perspective is widespread, academic administrators will need to go beyond a discussion of pertinent legal issues in order to encompass the professional and ethical responsibilities of faculty members as well.

Penalties for Academic Dishonesty

The courts have long regarded the imposition of discipline in an educational setting to be part of "the teaching process" (*Goss*, 1975, p. 583; see also *Mary M.*, 1984). Students learn that they are responsible for their actions, and that a serious offense deserves a serious sanction, both for reasons of deterrence, and as a matter of justice. Furthermore, the disciplinary process at institutions of higher education can and should be associated with ethical dialogue, and with penalties which are designed to promote moral growth and development.

Some academic administrators may believe that educational values and the imposition of discipline are incompatible. The courts certainly do not share such an assumption. For example, after reviewing an academic dishonesty case at Princeton University, an appellate court in New Jersey observed that deterrence was a valid justification for punishment in a campus environment, and that such punishment had a valid "educational effect:"

> Plaintiff claims that the penalty is supposed to provide something educative in its imposition. She argues that the penalty here is improper because there is no educational value to be found in it. Perhaps the plaintiff's self-concern blinds her to the fact that the penalty imposed on her, as a leader of the University community, has to have some educative effect on other student members of the community. In addition, to paraphrase the poet, "the child is mother to the woman," we believe that the lesson to be learned here should be learned by Gabrielle Napolitano and borne by her for the rest of her life. We are sure it will strengthen her in her resolve to become a success in whatever endeavor she chooses (*Napolitano*, 1982, p. 279).

Holding students accountable for acts of academic dishonesty can have significant deterrent value, especially if the campus community is informed on a regular basis of the number and types of cases, and the penalties imposed. The educational value of sanctions, however, is not limited to promoting a cost/benefit analysis on the part of the students who might be tempted to engage in academic dishonesty. An even more important objective associated with the imposition of discipline is the affirmation of values which promote community life, and the moral growth of individuals.

A 1984 report of the Study Group on Conditions of Excellence in American Higher Education contained the observation that "every college has a distinct culture—nonverbal messages that students pick up from virtually every aspect of campus life" (*Chronicle of Higher Education*, October 24, 1984, p. 40). One of the dangers associated with a failure to enforce academic dishonesty standards is that students learn the "non-verbal message" that the ethical values associated with academic integrity are not sufficiently important to merit any effort to enforce them. Some students may then be tempted to conclude that all values are transitory, and subordinate to the goals of acquiring wealth or power. This is precisely the conclusion which a University of Maryland student[4] seemed to reach in an interview published by the *Educational Record:*

Q. Do you feel that there is a problem with cheating at the university?

A. Undoubtedly.

Q. What have you seen? How bad is the situation? . . .

A. During one exam last month, I had the proctors standing right next to me talking to one another, saying how they were directed by the professor not to catch anybody cheating: "Don't. If you see somebody cheating, walk up from behind them, maybe they'll get scared and stop it. But it's a multiple choice exam and that's the sort of cheating that's too hard to prove, so don't even do it. Don't bother." Then the whole place was like a circus . . .

Q. Is [engaging in cheating] fair to [honest] students?

A. I don't think of it like that. I know some students do. But the attitude is generally, this is the way it is. When they work, a lot of these kids, either their fathers work in business, whatever they do, they get a shortcut—the other guy doesn't. That's the way I look at it. If I'm sharp enough to know the right people to get what I need, and he's not, then that's the point of the whole thing (1981, p. 27).

Student values emphasizing "shortcuts" in business and in the professions have been a matter of concern to the judiciary (See *North*, 1985: expulsion of medical student for fraud upheld; the "practice of medicine is not a simple matter of routine application of scientific principles . . . Physicians . . . must also possess a surpassing degree of ethical commitment" p. 147; See also *Clayton*, 1985, *Patterson* 1984). The courts assume that educational institutions have a major responsibility in "educating our youth for citizenship" and "teach(ing) by

[4]The student was subsequently expelled for academic dishonesty.

example the shared values of a civilized social order" (*Bethel*, 1986, p. 558). As Justice Powell has indicated, the imposition of just penalties in an academic setting is a necessary component of such an educational process:

> Education in any meaningful sense includes the inculcation of an understanding in each pupil of the necessity of rules and obedience thereto. This understanding is no less important than learning to read and write. One who does not comprehend the meaning and necessity of discipline is handicapped not merely in his education but throughout his subsequent life. In an age when the home and church play a diminishing role in shaping the character and value judgements of the young, a heavier responsibility falls upon the schools. When an immature student merits censure for his conduct, he is rendered a disservice if appropriate sanctions are not applied . . . (dissenting in *Goss* p. 593).

The judicial assumption that a just punishment can have a broadly educational function is entirely compatible with the theory of retribution. Essentially, retributive punishment affirms that there is a difference between right and wrong; that certain basic standards of moral behavior can be codified and enforced by the community; and that those who violate such standards should be held accountable for their actions. These views were best expressed by Herbert Morris in a prize winning essay appearing in *American Philosophical Quarterly*:

> [m]y point is that law plays an indispensable role in our knowing what for society is good and evil. Failure to punish serious wrongdoing . . . would only serve to baffle our moral understanding . . ..
>
> Further . . . punishment, among other things, permits purgation of guilt and ideally restoration of damaged relationships. Punishment, then, communicates what is wrong and in being imposed both rights the wrong and serves, as well, as a reminder of the evil done to others and to oneself in doing of what is wrong . . ..
>
> [Finally], the guilty wrongdoer is not viewed as damned by his wrongful conduct to a life forever divorced from others. He is viewed as a responsible being, responsible for having done wrong and possessing the capacity for recognizing the wrongfulness of his conduct (1981, p. 268).

The imposition of sanctions for reasons of deterrence or retribution does not require the automatic application of Draconian penalties. Indeed, penalties which are perceived as being too severe may actually inhibit the reporting of academic dishonesty cases, or discourage hearing boards from finding students guilty of an offense, even if the evidence warrants such a conclusion. These are common problems associated with those traditional "single sanction" honor codes which mandate expulsion for any act of dishonesty.

Perhaps the best example of the most effective use of the traditional "single sanction" of expulsion[5] is the Honor System at the University of Virginia. Even at Virginia, however, a policy evolved that only "reprehensible" violations should result in a guilty verdict. In 1984, the president of the university expressed particular concern about the effect of such a policy, after a student "who had been convicted and sentenced in a criminal court" for embezzlement "was subsequently acquitted in an Honor System trial . . ." (Hereford, 1984, p. 3). Virginia has now replaced the "reprehensibility" standard with a requirement that an act must be "a serious enough breach of trust to warrant permanent expulsion" before there can be a finding of guilt (*On My Honor* . . . p. 6). Nontheless, the potential effect of the "seriousness" standard seems much the same. The temptation will remain to find students "not guilty" of offenses which might legitimately merit a sanction less than expulsion. Students excused under these circumstances may then draw the unfortunate conclusion that minor acts of academic dishonesty, as "redefined according to contemporary standards of each generation of students" (*On My Honor* . . ., p. 6) will somehow be acceptable.

For the most part, any shortcomings in traditional honor codes are mitigated by the fact that many honor code schools are at least willing to impose serious penalties in serious cases of intentional academic fraud.[6] The practice at many other institutions of simply requiring a student to redo an assignment, or dropping a letter grade in a course, trivializes even the more flagrant forms of academic dishonesty. Such lenient penalties, like penalties which are perceived as being too strict, discourage the reporting of cases, and may ultimately discredit an entire institutional program to protect academic integrity.

Most institutions of higher education will wish to develop penalties which fall somewhere between a reduced course grade and expulsion,

---

[5]The penalty of "expulsion" at some traditional honor code schools, including Virginia, may have less substance than meets the eye. See the University of Virginia publication *On My Honor* p. 3):

> When a student is found guilty of an honor offense and is asked to leave the University, no moral judgement is made saying he is a bad person. No notation is made upon his transcript denoting that he has been dismissed, and he is provided with assistance in gaining admission to another institution if he requests such aid.

One observer has suggested that "expulsions" of this nature have only a limited impact, given the fact that an expelled student is thrown to a "pack of ravenous admissions officers from other Universities" (Amsden, 1977, p. 41).

[6]Imposing significant sanctions is by no means an easy task, as can be seen by the experience of Woodrow Wilson when he was President of Princeton University. When Wilson expelled a student for an honor code violation, the student's mother pleaded for her son's reinstatement:

> She said she was undergoing serious medical treatments and that the shock of having her boy expelled might well bring those treatments to naught. The answer was, "Madam, you force me to say a hard thing, but if I had to choose between your life or my life or anybody's life and the good of this college, I should choose the good of this college." But [Wilson] could eat nothing at luncheon that day. (Smith, 1964, p. 28).

at least for first offenders. Generally, it is more effective to impose moderate sanctions in a larger number of academic dishonesty cases than to subject only a very few students to the most severe punishment (see, e.g. Wilson and Herrnstein, 1985, p. 398: "[i]ncreasing the severity of a penalty without also increasing its certainty has little effect on behavior"). One reasonable penalty used at a number of institutions is a presumptive suspension. This means that students found responsible for academic dishonesty, even for a first offense, would have a burden of convincing the decision-maker that there are specific and significant mitigating factors which should result in a lesser penalty. For example, the absence of advance planning might be such a mitigating factor, since a student who simply glanced at another student's paper during an examination would be less deserving of being suspended than a student who prepared and brought a "crib" sheet to the examination room. The greater degree of calculated disregard for standards of academic integrity in the latter case is the reason for the more serious penalty.

Another appropriate penalty in academic dishonesty cases might be a recorded grade of XF. Such a grade would appear on a student's transcript with the notation "failure due to academic dishonesty" (see, e.g. University of Delaware disciplinary policies, 1987; see also *Newsweek*, May 26, 1980, p. 64; "Professors at the University of Pennsylvania give an X grade to a student caught cheating—worse than an F on the transcript because of what it signifies"). The XF transcript notation will have deterrent value, and might reasonably be regarded as being more severe than an "expulsion" which is not recorded on a student's academic records. Accordingly, for most first offenders, it seems appropriate to provide a means by which the XF can be removed and replaced with a grade of F, without any permanent transcript notation related to academic dishonesty. For example, the proposed *Code of Academic Integrity* (set forth in Appendix Two) provides that an XF may be removed by majority vote of a "Student Honor Council," after a student found accountable for an offense has successfully completed a required seminar on academic integrity.

Regardless of whether an XF grade penalty is adopted, a required, non-credit seminar on academic integrity would represent an effort to draw upon the educational resources of a college or university in order to foster lasting changes in student behavior. This approach is consistent with the overall mission of an institution of higher education, and is likely to be viewed with considerable favor by the courts (see, e.g. *General Order*, 1968, p. 137: Missions of tax supported institutions of higher education include helping to "develop, refine, and teach ethical and cultural values;" see also *Ambach*, 1986, cited in *Bethel*, 1986, p. 557: objectives of public education include teaching the "fundamental values necessary to the maintenance of a democratic political system."). Such a seminar would need to go beyond "values clarification" and seek to affirm certain fundamental virtues, including many of the virtues implicit in adherence to the scientific method (see, e.g. Eddy, 1977, p. 14: "to listen honestly and tolerantly to evidence from whatever source, to entertain alternative points of view with respect, to engage in self-judgment and self-criticism, and to abandon results that gratify the ego but simply aren't true."). In this regard, the subject matter of the seminar would be consistent with a growing consensus that there are certain normative values "about which [secular] society and all religions are in basic agreement: personal responsibility, honesty, self-discipline, and other qualities of character" (Welsh, 1986, p. 8; see also Lamm, 1986, p. 35: "to be value-neutral means to abandon the very premise on which the search for knowledge is pursued. If the University does not teach the moral superiority of . . . integrity as against cheating—then its very foundations begin to crumble").

It will not be necessary to resort to sermons or an exchange of moral homilies in order to affirm the values of academic integrity. Educators can rely instead upon ethical dialogue (Pavela, 1985, 1986) and the use of provocative case studies in order to foster ethical thinking, and what is likely to be a broad consensus as to the importance of pursuit of truth (see, e.g. *New York Times*, November 16, 1987, p. 54: account of Wesleyan University Professor Philip Hallie's "emphasis on 'flesh and blood' people" confronting moral dilemmas and issues). There is recent research suggesting that such techniques can produce at least "modest gains in moral reasoning" (*Harvard Education Newsletter*, January, 1987, p. 2). Moreover, even if immature students do not appear to be prepared to advance immediately to higher "stages"[7] of moral reasoning, sufficiently provocative case studies and experiences certainly can be remembered and assimilated later in life.

If a case study approach is to be used in an academic integrity seminar, course instructors might be advised to provide a number of examples involving ethical issues in business and finance. Relatively large numbers of students are seeking careers in those fields (see *New York Times*, January 12, 1987, p. A15: "one college freshman in four is preparing for a career in business . . . A record 73 percent of students listed 'being well off financially' as a top goal"). An important factor

[7]See Kohlberg, 1971, and Perry, 1981. For a contrasting point of view consider Coles, 1986:
> I've said 'Goodbye!' to American secular social science, and a lot of other things in the American secular world, which is hungry for certitudes, and formulations, and stages and phases, and wants everything categorized and put into labels and compartments, and wants an explanation and a recommendation for when you take your next breath, wants to be told at what day and what month and what year a child should learn how to read, and how to have sex 150 new ways, and lose weight, and keep your cholesterol at a certain level, and you can't even die without these people telling you the stages you're supposed to go through!

which such students might consider is that the practice of business in a comparatively free economy is heavily dependent upon voluntary adherence to a number of important ethical values (see Adam Smith, cited in Novak, 1982, p. 147: "In the race for wealth . . . he may run as hard as he can . . . in order to outstrip all his competitors. But if he should jostle or throw down any of them, the indulgence of the spectators is entirely at an end. It is a violation of fair play, which they cannot admit of;" see also Rosenberg and Birdzell, 1986). Failure to adhere to those values results in more governmental regulation (Edwards, 1987). Furthermore, students who aspire to leadership positions in business or government need to be aware of recent studies which have found that qualities such as "honesty" and "credibility" are "almost always" used to describe the attributes of the "most admired" executives and managers (Kouzes, 1987, p. F3). In short, for many individuals, the practice of business can become a means to develop character, as well as a way to earn a living (Solomon and Hanson, 1985). Those who view business solely as a means of acquiring wealth may find that financial success, standing alone, is a "disappointment, an ending" (Berglass, 1986, p. 1; see also LaBier, 1986). One of the most important functions of an academic integrity seminar would be to encourage the participants to understand that the relentless pursuit of material gratification is likely to be self-defeating. Instead, productive work, the ability to love, and an openness to the possibility of a broader meaning in life offer a richer and more satisfactory sense of happiness.[8]

In addition to prescribing an academic integrity seminar for first offenders, the proposed *Code of Academic Integrity* provides for significant student involvement in resolving academic dishonesty cases, and in imposing appropriate penalties. One reason for such a policy is that the threat of punishment alone is not likely to produce a lasting change in student behavior. In order to reach that objective, campus officials need to foster support for academic integrity within the student peer group. Such support is much more likely to be forthcoming if students perceive that they are actively involved in formulating the standards and procedures by which they will be governed. Given the natural interest which students have in the reputation of the educational institutions they are attending, it is unlikely that they would use whatever authority is granted to them in order to undermine a process designed to protect academic integrity, and the quality of their degrees. (See, e.g. Connell, 1981, p. 22).

---

[8]See Solzhenitsyn, 1980, p. 19:
> [s]ince his body is doomed to death, [man's] task on earth evidently must be more spiritual; not a total engrossment in everyday life, not the search for the best ways to obtain material goods and then their carefree consumption. It has to be the fulfillment of a permanent earnest duty so that one's life journey may become above all an experience of moral growth: to leave life a better human being than one started it.

Student participation in resolving allegations of academic dishonesty is also of immediate educational value to those individuals who are directly involved in reporting or resolving cases. Former President Hereford at the University of Virginia observed in this regard that "countless alumni have stated that the responsibility they held as students to sustain a community of trust gave them a deep, lifelong regard for integrity." (Hereford, 1984, p. 3). It is this type of responsibility which former Chief Justice Burger may have had in mind when he observed in *Healy*, that "(p)art of the educational experience of every college student should be an experience in responsible self government" (1972, p. 195, concurring opinion). By creating a "Student Honor Council," the proposed *Code of Academic Integrity* would provide such an experience to relatively large numbers of participants.

Finally, it should be emphasized that none of the policies suggested in this section will be of any enduring value if faculty and staff members do not adhere to the standards of integrity which they set for others. Students are uncannily adept at sensing hypocrisy; they know cognitively and intuitively that the actual practices of an institution of higher education are the most accurate reflection of the institution's philosophy. Misleading statements in official publications, the awarding of inflated grades in order to encourage higher enrollments, fraud in campus athletic programs, and other forms of impropriety, will make a mockery of official pronouncements encouraging the student body as a whole to adhere to high standards of academic integrity. The end result will be pervasive cynicism, and the antithesis of what a college or university education is designed to accomplish.

CONCLUSION

Academic dishonesty is regarded as being an offense which is disciplinary in nature, although its control is essential to the academic enterprise, and to academic administration. Basic due process protections should be provided when students are accused of academic dishonesty, although the nature of the due process may differ from that applied in other forms of discipline. In any event, complex, trial-type procedures with participation by counsel should be avoided, both to insure that allegations are resolved promptly and appropriately, and because students are often disadvantaged by adversarial proceedings in an educational environment. Faculty members who report academic dishonesty cases have little to fear in terms of personal liability, since the law accords them "some degree of immunity," provided that reports are made in good faith, in accordance with reasonable campus procedures, and are not shared with individuals who have no legitimate interest in the case. Any penalties which are imposed in academic dishonesty cases should have significant deterrent value, and must be proportionate to the offense. Penalties which are either too strict or too lenient will discourage the reporting of cases. Careful consideration should be given to an *XF* grade penalty, coupled with a required academic integrity seminar. Finally, no policy designed to protect academic integrity is likely to be successful without significant student participation, and a willingness by faculty and staff members to adhere to the ethical standards which they set for others.

Appendix I

Developing a Program to Protect Academic Integrity[1]

1. One of the most effective ways to promote academic integrity would be to enhance the quality of intellectual life on campus. Faculty and staff members who encourage critical thinking, and who actively engage students in dialogue and discussion, will create a climate in which academic fraud is unlikely to flourish.

2. Whenever possible, academic administrators should endeavor to avoid large, anonymous, lecture-style classes in which it is virtually impossible for faculty members to know and interact with students. Research indicates that academic dishonesty is far less likely to occur in small classes where there is a significant, positive relationship between students and teachers.

3. In the broadest sense, reducing and controlling academic dishonesty entails improving the campus environment for students. Perhaps the most important ingredient in such an effort would be fostering an appreciation of the college or university as a community of shared values. The willingness to affirm and enforce such values helps students to develop a sense of moral direction and to accept the responsibility to make a constructive contribution to community life. In practical terms, this means establishing a strict but fair standard of conduct for students, faculty, and staff members, and enforcing that standard in an equitable manner.

4. The affirmation of shared community values requires active participation by students, especially in developing and enforcing standards pertaining to academic integrity. It is for this reason the model *Code of Academic Integrity*, set forth in Appendix II provides for a Student Honor Council. The Council is empowered to appoint

---

[1]A different version of this document appears in an earlier publication. See Gehring, Nuss, and Pavela (1986).

student members to an institutional hearing panel, and other duties specified in Part 12 of the *Code*. An important objective in establishing a Student Honor Council is to encourage support for academic integrity within the student peer group. Since members of the Honor Council would be appointed by a broad range of campus student organizations, it is reasonable to expect that those organizations would devote at least some time on an annual basis to academic integrity issues. This system will require regular, careful, and attentive management by campus administrators, and also provides for significant faculty involvement. Nonetheless, active participation by students is consistent with their role in the larger society, since many students could sit on a jury even in the most serious criminal cases. Furthermore, since students are genuinely interested in the reputation of the institution from which they plan to graduate, it can be anticipated that they will be willing to support the implementation of equitable penalties in academic dishonesty cases.

5. Procedures might be developed to assess the quality of student performance prior to graduation. A properly administered comprehensive examination, or senior thesis, could enhance the overall educational experience for students and discourage students from engaging in long term patterns of academic fraud.

6. Faculty and staff members should aspire to adhere to the fundamental ethical ideals which they expound to students. For example, misleading statements in institutional publications, or fraud and abuse in campus athletic programs, will make a mockery of official pronouncements encouraging the student body as a whole to adhere to high standards of academic integrity.

7. Vigorous and consistent efforts should be made to reduce obvious temptations to engage in academic dishonesty. It is important to understand that inadequate proctoring, the unnecessary use of take-home examinations, and the careless distribution of official forms and documents may needlessly tempt otherwise decent students to be dishonest.

8. Faculty, staff, and student representatives should be asked to develop clear and consistent definitions for academic dishonesty which will be followed throughout the campus.

9. Penalties for academic dishonesty must go beyond a simple grade penalty in the course. For example, the model *Code of Academic Integrity*, set forth in Appendix II, would provide for a grade of XF, designated on the transcript as a finding that the student had engaged in academic fraud. The XF grade, patterned after penalties developed at the University of Delaware, could be removed from the transcript in accordance with standards and procedures published in advance. Also, consideration should be given to a policy of

suspending students found responsible for academic dishonesty, unless specific and significant mitigating factors are present.

10. Procedures for resolving allegations of academic dishonesty must be simple and equitable. Technical rules of evidence, active participation by lawyers, and formal appeals are not necessary.

11. The institution's explicit commitment to academic integrity, along with a statement of relevant policies and procedures, should be widely disseminated within the campus community. Such dissemination might include—

    a. A statement of policy pertaining to academic integrity in the application for admission. The policy statement might be signed by each applicant.

    b. A detailed pamphlet containing relevant institutional policies, with specific examples of academic dishonesty.

    c. Personal discussions and sharing of written policies at freshman and transfer orientation. Special efforts should be made to advise international students.

    d. Publication of relevant institutional policies on the front cover of official examination booklets, in the schedule of classes, the faculty handbook, and in the catalogue.

    e. Placing regular announcements about institutional standards pertaining to academic integrity in the campus press, especially at the beginning of school and during examination times.

    f. Annual correspondence to faculty members, teaching assistants and student leaders detailing institutional efforts to reduce academic dishonesty, reporting appropriate data or examples, suggesting improvements in policies or procedures, and stressing the importance of ongoing efforts to protect academic integrity.

12. Regular efforts should be made to recognize faculty members who properly report cases of academic fraud. Even a simple letter of appreciation, signed by the dean or academic vice president and placed in the faculty member's file, will be at least some acknowledgement of the time and energy which the faculty member devoted to the matter.

13. Appropriate assistance should be available to any faculty member asked to appear before a hearing panel. For example, at some institutions, a part-time legally-trained "Campus Advocate" is employed to assist faculty members in gathering and presenting evidence. However, in order to avoid unnecessary legalism, the Campus Advocate should not be asked to "represent" the faculty member at a hearing, unless the accused student is allowed legal representation.

14. Faculty members must be informed about institutional policies and should be given practical advice as to how to prevent academic dishonesty. It would be best if such information were made available in the faculty handbook and specifically called to the attention of each new faculty member.

15. Faculty members will also need advice as to how to conduct themselves when they observe academic dishonesty. Specific examples and suggestions might be set forth in the faculty handbook.

16. A convenient means should be available for students to report academic dishonesty. Several campuses use a telephone "hotline" for this purpose. Anonymous reports might be accepted, but disciplinary action should not be based on anonymous reports alone. Prompt written reports of each telephone contact should be forwarded to the chair of the appropriate academic department. Such a practice would enable administrators to detect apparent patterns of academic dishonesty in particular courses.

17. A specific individual or office should be responsible for coordinating efforts to reduce and control academic dishonesty. The occasional "reform" efforts on some campuses (usually engendered in the aftermath of a widely publicized incident) are dissipated as time passes and as attention is devoted to other problems. The effective control of academic dishonesty requires regular monitoring of relevant data, analysis of the effectiveness of institutional policies and procedures, and frequent communication with faculty, staff and students.

18. The deterrent effect of punishment is lost if the community is unaware of the penalties which are imposed for academic dishonesty. Regular announcements of case results should be published in the campus press, with all identifying information deleted.

Appendix II

Code of Academic Integrity

Prepared by Gary Pavela

PREFACE

This document is designed to incorporate many features of a traditional honor code into an administrative structure which also provides for significant faculty and staff participation. Academic integrity is a legitimate concern for every member of the campus community; all share responsibility for development and enforcement of appropriate policies and procedures. Although there are many ways of sharing that responsibility, the approach set forth in the draft Code is to give considerable discretion to faculty and staff members in reporting and processing allegations of academic dishonesty. In turn, the exercise of faculty and staff discretion is checked, structured and complimented by a Student Honor Council. Such balancing and sharing of authority is premised upon an assumption that control of academic dishonesty will not be accomplished by the threat of punishment alone. Ultimately, the most effective deterrent will be a commitment to academic integrity within the student peer group. Only by giving students genuine responsibility in a collaborative effort with faculty and staff members can such a commitment be fostered and maintained.

CODE OF ACADEMIC INTEGRITY

Academic dishonesty is a serious offense at the university because it undermines the bonds of trust and honesty between members of the community and defrauds those who may eventually depend upon our knowledge and integrity. Such dishonesty consists of:

Cheating

Intentionally[1] using or attempting to use unauthorized materials, information, or study aids in any academic exercise[2]

Fabrication

Intentional and unauthorized falsification or invention of any information or citation in an academic exercise.[3]

Reference footnotes under Commentary beginning on p. 75

Facilitating Academic Dishonesty

Intentionally or knowingly helping or attempting to help another to violate any provision of this *Code*.[4]

Plagiarism[5]

Intentionally or knowingly representing the words or ideas of another as one's own in any academic exercise.

Procedures

1. A faculty member who suspects that a student has committed an act of academic dishonesty shall:

    (a) so inform the student and [a designated administrative officer] in writing on the standard form established for that purpose;[6] and

    (b) if authorized by [the administrative officer], accord the student an opportunity for a personal meeting to discuss the allegation and to present relevant evidence, in accordance with procedures set forth in part 3 of this *Code*.

2. Prior to authorizing a faculty member to resolve a case, [the designated administrative officer] shall agree to meet with an accused student, upon the student's timely request, in order to review pertinent procedures. In any event, [the designated administrator] will retain discretionary authority to refer a case for a hearing, to modify or clarify the charges, or to hear the case informally, consistent with the procedures and sanctions specified for cases resolved by faculty members, as set forth in parts 3-5. Hearing referrals may be made in contested or complicated cases, or upon the faculty member's request, or for other good cause. A referral to a hearing must be made if a student is subject to suspension or expulsion,[7] or in any case in which a student makes a timely written request for a hearing. A request for a hearing will be timely if submitted in writing within ten business days after a student was given the notice required in part 1 (a) of this *Code*, either by personal delivery or by certified mail.[8]

3. Proceedings in cases resolved by a faculty member, as specified in part 1 (b) of this *Code*, are informal and nonadversarial. The faculty member will provide the student with written notice of a scheduled meeting at least three days in advance. The purpose of the meeting will be to review and discuss the charges before a final decision is reached. Documentary evidence and written statements could be relied upon by the faculty member, as long as the student was allowed to respond to them at the meeting. Students may also be allowed to bring relevant witnesses, or be accompanied by parents or other advisors, in the sole discretion of the faculty member. Neither the faculty member nor the student will be represented by legal counsel.

Reference footnotes under Commentary beginning on p. 75

4. A faculty member who is authorized to hear the case in accordance with part 3, and who determines that a student is responsible for an act of academic dishonesty, may take any of the following actions,* which shall be promptly reported in writing to [the designated administrative officer], along with a brief written statement of reasons for finding the student responsible for the offense:
   (a) impose additional course requirements, including repetition of the work in question;
   (b) impose a grade of *F*;
   (c) impose a grade of *XF*, as specified in part 10 of this *Code*.
   A student found responsible for any act of academic dishonesty will also be left with a disciplinary record, which shall be maintained in accordance with policies established for all disciplinary cases. The record may be voided if the student successfully completes the university sponsored academic integrity seminar, as specified in part 10 of this *Code*, and is not found responsible for any subsequent disciplinary offense.
5. Except for the *XF* grade penalty, penalties imposed in accordance with parts 2 and 4 of this *Code* shall be final and conclusive and not subject to appeal within the university disciplinary system.
6. Students subject to the *XF* penalty, when imposed in accordance with parts 2 and 4 of this *Code*, may file a timely appeal with the Student Honor Council. An appeal will not be timely if it is received more than ten business days after the student has been given written notice of the penalty, either by personal delivery or certified mail. The Student Honor Council will consider only written appeals, in accordance with the following standards—
   (a) The *XF* penalty may be rescinded if it is determined to be grossly disproportionate to the offense.
   (b) The case may be remanded for a hearing, in accordance with parts 7 and 8, if a deviation from the procedures specified in this *Code* were so substantial as to deny the student the fundamental requirements of due process, as defined by the courts in cases of academic discipline at institutions of higher education.
7. Students referred for a hearing shall be so notified in writing either by personal delivery or by certified mail, and will be provided with a statement specifying the charge(s). Students referred for a hearing are subject to the full range of disciplinary sanctions, including suspension or expulsion, as well as the penalties specified in part 4 of this *Code*.
8. The following procedural guidelines are applicable in academic dishonesty hearings—

---

*Some campuses may wish to mandate a single sanction of *XF*.

(a) Students shall be informed of the hearing date and the specific charges against them at least ten days in advance.

(b) Cases shall be resolved by a hearing board administered by the [chief academic or student affairs officer]. The board will include two faculty members appointed by the [designated administrative officer][9] and three members of the student honor council, as provided in part 12 of this *Code*. An ad hoc board composed of two students and one faculty member may be selected by [the designated administrative officer] if it is determined that a regular hearing board cannot be convened in time to resolve a pending case promptly.

(c) A non-voting hearing officer will preside. Hearing officers shall exercise control over the proceedings to avoid needless consumption of time and to achieve the orderly completion of the hearing.

(d) The accused student may be assisted by an advisor, who may be an attorney.[10] The role of the advisors will be limited to:
  (1) making a brief, relevant opening statement;
  (2) suggesting relevant questions which will be directed by the hearing officer to any witnesses;
  (3) providing confidential advice to the accused student;
  (4) making a brief, relevant statement as to any appropriate sanction to be imposed.

(e) The complainant shall be an administrative officer, designated by the university, who may not be a licensed attorney, or a law school graduate.

(f) Hearings will be closed to the public, except for the immediate members of the accused student's family and for the accused student's advisor. An open hearing may be held, in the discretion of the hearing officer, if requested by the accused student.

(g) Any person, including the accused student, who disrupts a hearing or who fails to adhere to the rulings of the hearing officer may be excluded from the proceeding.

(h) Hearings shall be tape recorded or transcribed.

(i) Prospective witnesses, other than the complainant and the accused student, may be excluded from the hearing during the testimony of other witnesses. All parties, the witnesses, and the public shall be excluded during panel deliberations.

(j) The burden of proof shall be upon the complainant, who must establish the guilt of the accused student by clear and convincing evidence.

(k) Formal rules of evidence shall not be applicable. The hearing officer shall give effect to the rules of confidentiality and privilege, but shall otherwise admit all matters into evidence which reasonable persons would accept as having probative

---

Reference footnotes under Commentary beginning on p. 75

value in the conduct of their affairs. Unduly repetitious or irrelevant evidence may be excluded.

(l) Accused students shall be accorded an opportunity to question those witnesses who testify for the complainant at the hearing.

(m) Affidavits shall not be admitted into evidence unless signed by the affiant and witnessed by a university employee.

(n) A determination of guilt shall be followed by a supplemental proceeding in which either party may submit evidence or make statements concerning the appropriate sanction to be imposed. The past disciplinary record of the accused student shall not be supplied to the panel prior to the supplementary proceeding.

(o) The final decision of the board shall be by majority vote.

(p) The board will provide a brief, written statement of reasons for finding a student responsible for an offense.

9. The decision of the hearing board will be a recommendation to the [chief academic or student affairs officer]. Students will be provided with a copy of the board's decision by personal delivery or by certified mail, and will have five business days after receiving the decision to provide written comments to the [chief academic or student affairs officer]. Subsequent action taken by the [chief academic or student affairs officer] shall be final and conclusive and not subject to further appeal within the university disciplinary system.

10. The *XF* grade penalty specified in part 4 (c) shall be recorded on the transcript with the notation "failure due to academic dishonesty." The *XF* symbol may be removed, and permanently replaced with a grade of *F*, upon the student's written petition to the Student Honor Council. Such a petition may not be granted if the student has been found responsible for any other disciplinary offense, and will not be granted until the student has successfully completed a regularly scheduled non-credit seminar on academic integrity and moral development.* All other student records pertaining to academic dishonesty will be voided in accordance with procedures established for student disciplinary cases. No student with the *XF* grade on the transcript will be permitted to represent the university in any extra-curricular activity, or run for or hold office in any recognized student organization.

11. A reasonable administrative fee, as established by the Student Honor Council and approved by [a designated administrative officer], will be charged to students found responsible for academic dishonesty, or other comparable disciplinary offenses. The Student Honor council may waive the fee, and substitute a community service assignment, upon petition.

---

*The *XF* penalty and the academic integrity seminar are derived from current policies at the University of Delaware.

12. A student honor council consisting of twelve members shall be established. Seven members of the council will be appointed by those campus honorary societies and organizations designated by the [chief academic officer], in consultation with the president of the student government association. Designated student organizations will include organizations representing commuter students, residential students, students residing in fraternities and sororities, and other organizations which promote racial, cultural, and other forms of diversity on campus. the five remaining members of the council shall be selected in accordance with procedures established by the [chief student affairs officer].

The honor council has the following powers and responsibilities:

(a) To develop its own bylaws and procedures, subject to approval by the [chief academic or student affairs officer] for legal sufficiency, and compliance with the standards set by this *Code*;

(b) to serve on and constitute the majority of the university hearing board, as specified in part 8 (b) of this *Code*. Appointments to the board shall rotate among honor council members, in accordance with council bylaws;

(c) to hear appeals from cases not referred to a hearing, as provided in part 6;

(d) to review and make final decisions concerning petitions by students for removal of the *XF* grade penalty, as specified in part 10 of this *Code*;

(e) to establish the administrative fee, and to consider fee waiver petitions, in accordance with part 11 of this *Code*;

(f) to modify the procedural guidelines established in part 8 of this *Code*, subject to approval by the [chief academic or student affairs officer] for legal sufficiency and compliance with the other standards set by the *Code*. Two-thirds vote of all twelve council members will be required before a proposed modification may be sent to [chief academic or student affairs officer] for final adoption;

(g) to review complaints of academic dishonesty which are either not referred to or not resolved by faculty members, in accordance with part 1. The review shall be conducted by a standing committee of three council members designated in accordance with council bylaws. If the standing committee determines that there is reasonable cause to believe that academic dishonesty may have occurred, the matter shall be referred to the [designated administrative officer], in accordance with part 2 of this *Code*. Council members who review any case in accordance with this part shall not participate in any subsequent proceedings pertaining to the case;

(h) assisting in design and teaching of the non-credit seminar specified in part 10 of this *Code*;

(i) advising and consulting with faculty and administrative officers on matters related to academic integrity standards, policies and procedures;

(j) issuing an annual report to the campus community on academic integrity standards, policies, and procedures, including recommendations for appropriate changes;

(k) additional duties or responsibilities delegated by the [chief academic or student affairs officer].

13. Both faculty members and students share concurrent authority for reporting allegations of academic dishonesty, in accordance with this *Code*. Faculty members must remain responsible for examination security, and the proctoring of examinations.

14. All applicants for admission to undergraduate or graduate programs at the university, as well as all students registering for courses, will be expected to write an honor pledge as a condition of admission.

COMMENTARY

The following footnotes reference copy beginning on page 69.

[1] Labeling a student as being "dishonest" constitutes a form of moral condemnation which can be a legitimate sanction in itself. Such moral condemnation, however, is not normally imposed for a simple act of negligence (e.g., a typographical error resulting in a miscited source). See *Wait* v. *University of Vermont*, unreported U.S. Civil Action 82-247 (D. Vt., 1982) p. 7:

> it is the accepted rule of law . . . that, before the imposition of civil or criminal liability for acts of deception or fraud, it must be shown that the actor either intended that his actions deceive, or acted with knowledge and reckless disregard of the possibility that his actions might deceive. This comports with the ordinary meaning of the words deceive, cheat, or defraud . . ..

The issue of "intent" is a question of fact. A student who cites long passages from a book without acknowledgement cannot expect to convince the decision-maker that the omission was merely "negligent." Also, requiring a showing of intent is not to be confused with excusing students who claim they were unaware of the rules. Such ignorance is not a valid defense. Not knowing what one has done (e.g., inadvertently omitting a footnote) is to be distinguished from knowingly doing something while ignorant of a rule.

[2] The term "academic exercise" includes all forms of work submitted for credit or honors at the University, as well as materials submitted to other institutions or organizations for evaluation or publication.

³ For example, a writer should not reproduce a quotation found in a book review and indicate that quotation was obtained from the book itself. Likewise, it would be improper to analyze one sample in a laboratory experiment and covertly "invent" data based on that single experiment for three more required analyses.

⁴ For example, one who provided term papers or examinations to other students while knowing or having reason to know that such materials would be used in violation of this *Code* would be responsible for "facilitating academic dishonesty."

⁵ The University subscribes to the statement on plagiarism which appears on page six of William Watt's *An American Rhetoric* (1955):

> The general principles for all honest writing can be summarized briefly. Acknowledge indebtedness:
>
> 1. Whenever you quote another person's actual words.
>
> 2. Whenever you use another person's idea, opinion or theory, *even if it is completely paraphrased in your own words.*
>
> 3. Whenever you borrow facts, statistics or other illustrative material—unless the information is common knowledge.

⁶ The form would contain a specific statement of facts to support the charge. Furthermore, the form would outline the policies and procedures of this *Code* and provide a list of student rights, including the right to request a hearing. Students should also be urged to meet with [the designated administrative officer] within five business days. Prominent notice shall be given to the ten-business-day time requirement for requesting a hearing.

⁷ Students who have been found responsible for previous disciplinary offenses may be in jeopardy of suspension or expulsion, as are students who have allegedly engaged in acts of dishonesty which required advance planning (e.g., preparing a crib sheet), considerable time or effort (e.g., extensive plagiarism) or cooperation with others (e.g., arranging in advance to share answers during an examination). Students subject to suspension or expulsion may waive a hearing by signing an appropriate waiver form. The form should contain an outline of the rights and procedures being waived, including any right of appeal, and specifically authorize [the designated administrative officer] to resolve the case and to impose any penalty authorized by this code. Students should be offered at least two business days to review the waiver form, and should also be invited to discuss the matter with an appropriate advisor or family member.

⁸ Certified mail will be considered delivered to the student if it is sent to the most recent address provided by the student to the Office of Records and Registrations, even if delivery is refused or the letter is unclaimed. Students should be advised of this policy in appropriate campus publications.

⁹ [The chief academic or student affairs officer] will select faculty members designated in advance by [pertinent academic units]. Although selection may be made on a case by case rotation basis, [the administrator] should retain discretion to make selections which will insure representation of appropriate academic disciplines, as necessary in each case.

¹⁰ A limitation upon participation by counsel is a natural outgrowth of the "investigatory" administrative hearing procedure set forth in this *Code*. Unlike the passive jury in the adversarial model, the hearing panel in an investigatory proceeding assumes much of the responsibility for questioning witnesses and eliciting relevant evidence. This system gives more active control of the case to the decision-maker, and diminishes the role of counsel. Properly used, it also protects the legitimate interests of the student respondent, since complainants should be subject to thorough questioning by the hearing panel members. The Supreme Court has permitted considerable leeway in the development of procedures of this nature, and held in *Matthews* v. *Eldridge* (424 U.S. 319, 348, 1976) that the traditional "judicial model is neither required, nor even the most effective method of decision making in all circumstances . . .." Finally, many experienced observers are convinced that one of the best reasons for limiting participation by counsel in student disciplinary cases is the damage which aggressive lawyers frequently inflict on their own clients. Many of the attorneys who do appear in campus proceedings practice criminal law, and have little or no experience in informal administrative hearings. As a result, they frequently resort to the histronics associated with jury trials and engage in excessive argumentation about "Miranda" warnings and other procedural requirements which have not been required in student conduct cases. These tactics often produce an adversarial climate which is not helpful to the accused student.

Appendix III

Case Studies[1]

CASE STUDY I — Susan Smith

Susan Smith, a junior, was enrolled in L-210, English Literature from 1600 to 1800, during fall semester 1985. Students in the class were required to complete three papers. The instructor had the students submit the topic of the paper at least three weeks prior to the due date.

Susan's second paper was turned in approximately one week after it was due. The instructor noticed that the topic was not the same one Susan had submitted earlier. Susan had previously indicated that she was going to write on a particular section of Milton's *Paradise Lost*. The paper which Susan submitted was on a section of the poem that was not in the anthology used in the course.

The instructor become suspicious and decided to have the references for the paper checked. Prior to checking the references, a former student, Peter, reported that Susan had asked to review a paper he had prepared for a graduate course on Milton.

Upon comparing the two papers the instructor determined that Susan had copied, with a few alterations, pages 1-15 and pages 24-25 of Peter's paper. The instructor asked the student to come to her office to discuss the matter. The instructor asked Susan if there was anything she wished to say about her paper, and she declined. The instructor then informed Susan that she believed the paper was plagiarized from Peter's paper. Susan denied the allegation.

At a subsequent hearing, Susan acknowledged that she had read Peter's paper, but said that it was only for ideas. As a defense to the

[1]These case studies and the suggested responses are not designed to serve as comprehensive descriptions or models. Instead, they are intended for use as initial starting points for discussion, analysis, and criticism in training exercises. Such exercises would be most effective if conducted with participation by diverse staff members. Case studies I and II were prepared by Ms. Nuss, case studies III and IV by Mr. Kibler and V and VI by Mr. Pavela.

plagiarism charge, Susan indicated that the reason the paper was late was because she was getting some assistance in finalizing the paper from a tutor in the campus writing center. She denied the charge of plagiarism.

A hearing panel found Susan responsible for plagiarism. She received an *F* in the course and was placed on disciplinary probation for one semester.

Comments

☐ While one might expect a junior to be familiar with the normal practices and definitions of plagiarism, it is always possible that a student does not understand how to give credit for the ideas of another. For these reasons it is important for instructors to discuss academic dishonesty at the beginning of each semester and to give examples of plagiarism and how to avoid unintentional infractions.

☐ The practice of requiring a student to submit the topic of the paper a few weeks prior to the due date can be an effective way of identifying possible cases of cheating or plagiarism which may take place when a student has not allowed adequate time to prepare the assignment.

☐ Students who seek help at a writing center or other tutorial assistance should understand the nature and scope of the assistance they receive. The tutor is likely to provide technical assistance without ascertaining whether or not the work is that of the individual student. However, in some cases the tutor may detect that the student is not sufficiently familiar or well versed in the subject and may suspect that plagiarism is a possibility. In all cases it is a good idea to have the staff at the tutorial centers well versed in the policies of academic integrity and to require that these policies are routinely reviewed with clients.

☐ In instances where students are found responsible for academic dishonesty, it is important that the hearing or disciplinary interview provide an opportunity for them to confront the implications of their behavior and understand how to avoid future occurrences. The student should also understand the terms and conditions of the probation status.

CASE STUDY II — Mary Beth & John

Mary Beth and John were both enrolled in a freshmen level linguistics class, F111. At the beginning of the semester the instructor, Dr. Jones, gave each student a statement on plagiarism and academic integrity. Dr. Jones stressed that turning in someone else's homework as though it were your own work is cheating. Dr. Jones reminded students that they may discuss the homework assignments with others but. . . "that everything you write down on paper must be your own answer explained in your own words." Students were told that cheating in F111 would be taken seriously. "The student who helps another student cheat is just as guilty as the student who used someone else's work."

On October 18, while grading homework, the graduate assistant noticed that two homework assignments including longer explanations of the material were exactly the same on all four pages of John's and Mary Beth's homework. The GA brought this to the attention of Dr. Jones who interviewed both students—at first separately and then together to determine the "whys" and "hows" of the duplicate work.

Admitting that John had helped her, Mary Beth was at first unable to define the nature of the help but when questioned more closely said John had given her some answers. John maintained that he had helped Mary Beth but had not given her any of his answers to the homework.

In follow-up conversations, John acknowledged giving Mary Beth the answers from his homework but said he was forced to because she had threatened to get him in trouble with his girlfriend if he didn't help her. John knew what he was doing was wrong, but feared that Mary Beth would make his girlfriend jealous and angry if he didn't give her the answers.

Both students were found responsible for cheating and received a grade of XF in the class. In addition Mary Beth was placed on disciplinary probation because the hearing panel believed she had harassed John into giving her the answers.

Comments

☐ This case highlights the fact that even when the policy on academic integrity has been carefully discussed in class some cheating may still occur. It is difficult to know what pressures or temptations prompted Mary Beth to cheat. Preventive measures are important but must be accompanied by appropriate disciplinary procedures and sanctions for violators.

☐ The role of peer pressure and the competing needs and values experienced by college-aged students can not be overlooked. John was aware that his actions were wrong and was capable of reasoning about the action. In this case his affiliation needs and the desire to keep peace with his girlfriend were of higher priority than the value of honesty. In spite of these pressures it is important for the disciplinary hearing to provide John with an opportunity to confront the implications of his behavior and to consider ways in which he might respond in future instances.

☐ Instructors should attempt to ensure that there are sufficient opportunities for students to be able to demonstrate their familiarity and competence with the course material throughout the semester. Undue reliance on one or two assignments may place considerable stress on a student. Students who believe there are multiple opportunities may not feel as much pressure to cheat on assignments.

CASE STUDY III — Debbie and Cindy

Prior to administering a test, Dr. Jones numbered all of the tests. After distributing all of the tests in the 2 p.m. section of Biology 101, Dr. Jones found that an extra test had been distributed. Making a visual count of the students taking the exam, he discovered that there was an extra person in the classroom.

Dr. Jones continued to proctor the exam carefully. As he walked around the classroom, he checked the names on the tests against the class roster. Upon finding a student who had not put her name on the test, Dr. Jones made note of the location of her seat in relation to surrounding students. During the remainder of the test period, he maintained a close watch on the unknown person and surrounding students. On three occasions, Dr. Jones suspected that Debbie may have been copying answers from the test of the unknown individual. Dr. Jones decided not to confront Debbie or the unknown person during the test, but wait until after the papers were graded. He expected to be able to show that the answers on Debbie's test were indeed copied from the test without a name.

After grading the tests, Dr. Jones found that the answers on Debbie's test appeared to be copied from the test without a name. The manner in which the problems were worked had not been covered in class. Based on Debbie's past performance, it was doubtful that she would have used this complicated method.

Dr. Jones called Debbie to his office to discuss with her the allegation of copying from a neighbor. When confronted with the facts, Debbie admitted to copying from the neighbor to her right, the unknown individual. Dr. Jones asked her to identify this individual. At first Debbie was very reluctant to reply. She said that she was pledging a sorority and was worried about making her grades so that she could become an active member. Her big sister in the sorority had taken the class from another professor and had offered to help her. Initially, her big sister was just going to help her study for the test. Due to so much going on in the sorority, there just wasn't time to study so Debbie asked her big sister, Cindy, to sit next to her in class.

Appropriate disciplinary action was sought against both Debbie and Cindy in accordance with the university disciplinary process for cases involving academic dishonesty.

Prevention Strategies

☐ Have arranged seating for class on days tests are given. Keep the row to the left and the right of each student vacant.

☐ Utilize alternate test forms.

☐ Have students display their student picture ID cards on their desks during the test. Check name on ID card against class name on test.

☐ Have each student hand in test personally and show his/her ID when doing so. The instructor checks the name on the test against the ID card and verifies that the student is in that class by checking the class roster. The instructor then places his/her initials on the test.

CASE STUDY IV — Robert's Research Paper

Robert, a Political Science major, was in his final semester before graduation. It had been a very busy semester with job searching, planning a wedding to his high school sweetheart, and of course school work. Robert had just returned from an out of town interview. In two days, he had a major research paper due in Sociology 201. Because it was not a required course, he does not want to spend much time on the paper. Besides, he has a Political Science test at the end of the week.

Robert remembered that his hometown friend Steve took this class a year ago. Looking for an easy way out, Robert called Steve and asked him if he still had his research paper from Sociology 201. Steve said that he has kept all of his papers in his major classes. Robert told Steve that he would like to borrow the paper so he can get an idea of how to write one for Dr. Gonzalez. Steve agreed to lend Robert the paper for this purpose.

When Robert looked at Steve's paper, he realized that he would not have enough time to complete an acceptable research paper. Out of frustration, he decided to rewrite Steve's paper and submit it. As the time became shorter, the changes became fewer.

When Dr. Gonzalez was grading the research papers, he noticed that the style of writing in Robert's paper was different from previous examples of his writing. In fact, he seemed to recall a paper on the same topic written in some previous semester. Dr. Gonzalez compared Robert's previous work with the research paper noting differences in style and vocabulary. Because Dr. Gonzalez did not keep papers from previous semesters, he could not check on an earlier submitted paper.

Dr. Gonzalez called Robert to his office to discuss the findings. He confronted Robert with his belief that the paper included blatant examples of plagiarism. Robert replied that he had not copied any part of the paper word for word from any source. Dr. Gonzalez further explained what he meant by plagiarism citing examples of the variance in writing by Robert from previous papers.

It was suggested to Robert that his paper was quite similar to a paper submitted in a previous semester. Robert denied that he had knowledge of any other paper on the subject.

Comments

☐ Because there is not sufficient evidence, it cannot be shown that Robert was aware of another paper on the subject nor that he had plagiarized another student's paper.

☐ Limit the choice of topics given students and change the topics frequently.

☐ Have students submit an outline of the paper early on with a tentative bibliography. Require students to submit drafts of the paper with the final product.

☐ Give students a pop test or require an oral presentation prior to submitting the paper.

☐ Keep students' papers on file for five years.

☐ Use occasional in-class writing exercises to assess students writing ability.

CASE STUDY V — Dr. Smith and George

Dr. Smith, an accounting professor, requires the students in her classes to turn in homework problems at regular intervals for grading. The homework problems are in the accounting workbook that accompanies the text. It is an expectation that each student has his/her own workbook. Homework is expected to be done independently although students may ask for help from fellow students or Dr. Smith herself.

A few days prior to the second homework assignment being due, Dr. Smith noticed a poster on the bulletin board in the classroom. The poster indicated that George was interested in purchasing the answers to the problems in the workbook. After class the professor returned to her office to see if George was in any of her classes. Dr. Smith discovered that the phone number on the poster was the same phone number listed for George Johnson in the campus directory. George Johnson was in Dr. Smith's 10 a.m. accounting class.

Is attempting to purchase answers to problems in an accounting workbook considered academic dishonesty when some of the problems are to be turned in for grading? How should Dr. Smith handle this situation?

Comments

☐ It may not be proper to assume that George was attempting to purchase the answers to workbook problems for the purpose of cheating on the homework assignment. Although coincidental timing would lead one to believe otherwise, George may have legitimate reasons for wanting the answers. For instance, George may plan to use the workbook to study for upcoming tests.

Assuming that George may be planning to use the purchased answers in preparing the homework problems for submission, there are different ways to approach the situation. If the professor wants to be proactive and preventive, she may call George to her office and confront him with the poster. Being careful not to unjustly accuse George of academic dishonesty, she may make him aware that it seems coincidental that the poster went up just prior to the date for submitting homework problems. She may indicate that she certainly hopes that George was not planning to utilize the purchased answers for this purpose. Finally, Dr. Smith must clarify that no disciplinary action is being considered unless the answers are used for illegitimate purposes.

A second approach is to wait to see if and how George may utilize the purchased answers. If in correcting the homework problems, Dr. Smith discovers that the work is not George's by comparing the methods with those on George's previous homework and by comparing with the methods taught in class, then proper disciplinary procedures should be followed.

Another issue in this case is whether the person who sold the answers to George committed an offense. It may be difficult to show that the seller was aware of the professor's policy unless the seller was a student of Dr. Smith. However, the seller may be found in violation of a university policy, if there is one, specifying that it is considered academic dishonesty if a student provides answers for any assigned work or examination when not specifically authorized to do so.

Comments

☐ The university should have a published policy that states that any act of providing or acquiring answers for any assigned work or examination, except when specifically authorized to do so, is considered academic dishonesty.

☐ The instructor should clearly set expectations concerning all forms of academic dishonesty, including acquiring information, the first week of classes. This information should be included in course sylabus.

☐ Keep copies of student's homework assignments during the semester.

CASE STUDY VI — John and Metad

John and Metad were devoted friends and collaborators. Unfortunately, one of their instructors at a public university suspected that their collaboration extended to cheating during a classroom examination. The course instructor became suspicious of John and Metad's activities at the outset of the examination, when she observed them sitting next to each other, contrary to her instructions to sit "every other seat." The instructor asked Metad to move, but noticed a few moments later that he had not done so. It was necessary for her to reiterate her instructions, and to point out a number of vacant seats.

Later, during the first portion of the examination, Metad walked to the front of the room to ask the instructor a question. She then observed him returning to his original seat next to John. Again, for a third time, she insisted that Metad sit in a different location.

The instructor decided to compare John and Metad's examination papers after the papers were submitted for grading. She discovered that both students' answers to fifty short answer questions were identical, including four wrong answers not commonly answered wrong by the rest of the class. Also, while both John and Metad had done A work on the short answer questions, neither student did very well on the essay portion of the examination, which covered the same material. Finally, the instructor noted over a dozen erasures on the short answer section of Metad's examination, which Metad stated had been done toward the end of the examination period.

Before reporting the matter to her dean, the instructor met privately and individually with John and Metad. Both asserted that they had not engaged in any form of cheating, and that the similarity of their short answer questions reflected the fact that they studied together. They also observed that their inferior performance on the essay portion of the examination was caused by the fact that neither has a history of doing well on essay examinations. Finally, Metad offered a number of reasons for his apparent determination to sit next to John during the examination. He asserted that the room was crowded, and vacant seats were not readily apparent. Furthermore, when he sat next to John a third time, he did so for "only two or three minutes" because he was "disoriented" and "not thinking or seeing clearly" due to "the pressure of the examination." His numerous erasures, in his view, proved his innocence, since they demonstrated that he was uncertain about his answers, and was concentrating on his own work.

The instructor told both students she was not persuaded by their responses. She told Metad in particular that she was disappointed in him, since he had told her what she regarded as an obviously false and contrived story. She then referred the case for a hearing, in accordance with campus policies.

Both John and Metad appeared at the hearing, which was held six weeks after the instructor referred the charge. Since the instructor was on sabbatical at the time, her written statement was submitted into evidence. John and Metad spoke for themselves, since their legal advisor was not allowed to address the hearing panel. The panel found both students guilty, by a "clear and convincing" standard of proof, although one panel member did vote for acquittal. Also, at the end of the hearing, one panelist reminded Metad that they had been high school classmates, and expressed regret at having to meet again under such unfortunate circumstances.

John and Metad were outraged! They raised the following issues in an appeal to the Dean—

1. The case against them was based solely upon circumstantial evidence. No one had seem them cheating, nor was any crib sheet found.

2. The instructor's comments to Metad about what she believed to be a contrived story were defamatory, insensitive, and abusive.

3. Due process standards were violated by:

   a) the faculty member's failure to appear at the hearing where she would have been subject to cross-examination;

   b) college policies restricting the role of legal counsel;

   c) absence of a "beyond a reasonable doubt" standard of proof;

   d) a policy permitting students to be found guilty by anything less than a unanimous vote;

   e) a biased hearing panel member, who had known Metad several years before.

   How should the dean respond?

Comments

☐ This case may provide some insight into the reluctance of many faculty members to report allegations of academic dishonesty. Such matters can become bitterly contested, and very time consuming. Although the first obligation of the campus administration is to insure that the accused students are treated fairly and reasonably, it will also be important to create a climate in which faculty members believe that their efforts are appreciated. Faculty members should not expect to "win" every case; nor should they take an adverse finding as a personal affront. However, it would be reasonable for faculty members to expect that honest and diligent efforts to protect academic integrity on campus will be properly recognized as a component of their "service" obligation to the institution.

☐ Circumstantial evidence which has probative value may be relied upon, even in a criminal case (Richardson, 1973, p. 117). For example, a hearing panel may properly draw inferences from the totality of evidence in order to conclude that "chance alone" would be "an extremely unlikely explanation" for suspicious patterns of answers on an examination (*McDonald*, 1974, pp. 102, 104). It is true that care should be taken in relying exclusively upon statistical evidence (see Buss and Novak, 1980, p. 14: "(a)ny limitations in the probative force of a statistical analysis to detect cheating are likely to be exacerbated if the statistical analysis provides the only evidence considered.") In the present instance, however, there are many other forms of evidence as well:

(1) virtually identical multiple choice answers, resulting in superior scores;

(2) contrasted with inferior responses to essays covering the same academic material;

(3) consistent and eventually successful efforts to sit in adjoining seats;

(4) such efforts being specifically prohibited by the instructor, requiring her repeated personal intervention;

(5) over a dozen answer sheet erasures by Metad, which he admits were accomplished sometime after he sat next to John during the examination.

Taken separately, each of these factors might be insufficient proof of academic dishonesty. In the aggregate, however, they are more than adequate to support the finding of the hearing panel, especially when one considers reasonable assessments of credibility, and Metad's implausible justifications for his repeated efforts to sit next to John.

In reaching this conclusion, one might rely upon the aphorism, "when offered a number of different theories, start with the simplest." The facts outlined above are most simply and logically explained by a theory which would encompass a finding of academic fraud. By contrast, John and Metad offer a somewhat baroque defense, based upon coincidence, improbable differences in performance upon the same examination, and Metad's stress-induced visual impairment (which, remarkably, did not affect his performance on the multiple choice portion of the examination).

Essentially, it is reasonable to conclude that both students, having reportedly studied together beforehand, also found it necessary to collaborate during the examination. Metad was almost certainly determined to sit near John in order to give or receive unauthorized assistance. Such assistance may have been prepared in advance, reduced to writing, designed to be shared, and initially held by John. This suggestion must remain a hypothesis, however, since the precise nature of the collaboration probably cannot be established with certainty. It is simply not possible to know "the intentions and thoughts" of individuals in these situations, "but such unattainable evidence is not required" (*Nash*, 1985, p. 959).

☐ The hearing panel came to the reluctant conclusion that John and Metad were not telling the truth about the nature of their activities during the examination. Making a determination of this nature is difficult and painful in a collegial setting. Nonetheless, while members of hearing panels must not assume that a student who is accused of academic dishonesty is likely to be lying, it will be essential to maintain a capacity for critical judgment, and to allow an honest and rigorous assessment of the facts to determine the outcome of the case. Experienced observers recognize the unpleasant reality that some individuals accused of academic dishonesty may seek to rely upon contrived and fabricated evidence, both to "prove" their innocence, and to discredit the accuser. Indeed, a number of current trends in our culture would appear to be exacerbating this problem. See Hesburgh, 1987, p. 55 ("To the extent family life is disintegrating, kids are not being taught values about lying, cheating, and stealing"). See also Bok, S. 1978, p. 257 ("many" individuals "who might be able to change the patterns of duplicity in their own lives lack any awareness of the presence of a moral problem in the first place, and thus feel no need to examine their behavior . . .. Others are beyond caring").

☐ A related problem which frequently arises in comparable cases is the hearing panel's ability to render a decision if some critical question depends upon assessment of "one person's word against another." Inexplicably, this issue seems to pose a special problem in the academic community, since faculty and staff members are occasionally paralyzed by indecision if a factual dispute cannot be resolved with mathematical certainty. Indeed, apparent violations of a wide variety of school regulations may go unreported, due to an assumption that more than one witness will be necessary. For example, see Grant, 1981:

> A female teacher was still shaking as she told us about a group of students who had . . . made sexually degrading comments about her in the hall. When we asked why she did not report them, she responded, "Well, it wouldn't have done any good." Why not? we pressed. "I didn't have any witnesses," she replied (p. 141; cited in D. Bok, 1983, p. 43).

It must be emphasized that it is possible to resolve a case even if two individuals give contradictory testimony about an issue in dispute. Members of the hearing panel should listen carefully, ask questions, consider the logical order and consistency of the testimony, evaluate the demeanor of the witnesses, and make a judgment.

College and university administrators need to understand that no judicial process can produce perfect justice. Indeed, even in a criminal case with a "beyond a reasonable doubt" standard of proof, there is a small risk that an innocent person may be convicted and punished. We reluctantly accept (and subject ourselves) to such a risk, because an even higher standard (e.g., proof of guilt "by a moral certainty") would make it virtually impossible for the community to protect itself. A careful balance between competing interests is necessary, and must be based upon a foundation of fundamental standards of fairness. The unavoidable fact is that close and difficult decisions simply cannot be avoided, even though we recognize the capacity for human error.

☐ Metad's argument about "defamatory" comments by the instructor does not appear to be accurate or relevant. Since Metad and the instructor were speaking privately, the teacher's expression of concern about Metad's "false and contrived story" cannot be defamatory, since it was not directed to or overheard by a third party. In any event, Metad needs to be reminded that the scope of the hearing was limited to resolution of the allegation of academic dishonesty. The issue of the alleged defamation was simply not relevant at the hearing, or on appeal.

Furthermore, Metad's concern about the instructor's comments reflects extraordinary and unjustified sensitivity. Complaints of this nature must not be allowed to inhibit staff members from speaking candidly with students. If the instructor believed Metad was lying to her, it was reasonable to raise the issue privately, and to explain to Metad why such behavior is likely to be self defeating. Also, it would be appropriate for the instructor to report the underlying facts of the case to campus officials responsible for academic integrity and student conduct, as provided by institutional regulations. Even if it were subsequently determined that some or all of the facts in the instructor's report were inaccurate, it is unlikely that the instructor could be found liable for defamation, unless the report were reckless, or motivated by malice (see, generally, Stevens, 1975).

Engaging students in dialogue and discussion about ethical issues can generate complaints that faculty and staff members are "judgmental" and "insensitive." What is truly insensitive, however, is the aura of benign, undifferentiated benevolence which too many educators use to disguise the exercise of authority. The latter practice has become a sophisticated bureaucratic art of survival which often enables college and university officials to avoid confrontations and quarrels; unfortunately, it also fails to help students define the boundaries by which they may shape their character.

☐ Most of John and Metad's due process arguments are unsupported by the caselaw. As outlined in the Legal Issues chapter, the courts are virtually unanimous in holding there is no legal right to the full and active participation of an attorney in a case involving academic discipline (Nash, 1985). Likewise, neither the "beyond a reasonable doubt" standard of proof, nor a unanimous verdict have been required by the courts in campus disciplinary proceedings (see Long, 1985; Nzuve, 1975). It is true, of course, that John and Metad are entitled to an unbiased hearing panel. However, the simple fact that one of the panel members knew Metad does not constitute sufficient proof of bias. It will be necessary for Metad to establish that the panel member was motivated by some sort of animosity toward him (Davis, 1972, p. 249). Even a panelist with a superficial knowledge of the background of the case need not be disqualified, provided that he or she can "judge the case fairly and solely on the evidence presented" (*Keene*, 1970, p. 222). However, hearing panel members who know the accused student, or who may be familiar with the facts of the case, should reveal such knowledge at the outset of a hearing, rather than at the end. Generally, if the accused student objects to the panelist's participation, it would be prudent to find a replacement.

John and Metad do raise a legitimate and important due process argument when they assert that they were unable to question the referring faculty member at the hearing. It is true that a series of cases has held that there is no constitutional right to cross-examination in college or university disciplinary proceedings. *Dixon*, 1961 ("This is not to imply that a full-dress judicial hearing, with the right to cross-examine witnesses, is required."); *Jaksa*, 1984 ("The Constitution does not confer on plaintiff the right to cross-examine his accuser in a school disciplinary hearing."); *Nash*, 1985 ("Neither the Fifth Circuit . . . nor the Supreme Court has expanded the rule in *Dixon* to require cross-examination and confrontation of witnesses in the context of school disciplinary proceedings . . ."). Nonetheless, judges recognize the value of cross-examination as an "essential and fundamental requirement for [a] fair trial" (*Pointer*, 1965, p. 405) and may require it if a college disciplinary case "resolved itself into a problem of credibility" (*Winnick*, 1972, p. 550); see also *Esteban*, 1969). As suggested in the Legal Issues chapter, application of the "Golden Rule" would be a useful guide in this context. If a faculty member or administrator would wish to cross-examine a person who had made a serious accusation against them, it would seem prudent and reasonable to accord a similar right to students.

In the present case, the inability of John and Metad to question the instructor does not necessarily mean that the findings should be reversed, or a new hearing conducted. The dean needs to undertake an honest assessment of the potential value of cross-examination before making a final decision. For example, if John and Metad do not deny the basic facts set forth in an affidavit by the instructor, cross-examination about unrelated issues (e.g., "defamation," or prior grading practices) would have "no bearing on the outcome of the hearing" and it would serve "no useful purpose " (*Winnick*, 1972, p. 549). These are difficult decisions for administrators to make; if there is a substantial doubt, it is usually

Table of Cases

Haynie v. Ross Gear Division of TRW, 799 F. 2d 237 (6th Cir., 1986).

Healy v. James, 408 U.S. 169 (1972).

Henson v. Honor Committee of University of Virginia, 719 F. 2d 69 (4th Cir., 1984).

Hill v. Trustees of Indiana University, 537 F. 2d 248 (7th Cir., 1976).

Jackson v. Dorrier, 424 F. 2d 213 (6th Cir., 1970).

Jaska v. Regents of University of Michigan, 597 F. Supp. 1245 (E.D. Mich., 1984).

Johnson v. Lincoln Christian College, 501 N.E. 2d 1380 (Ill. App., 1986).

Jones v. Board of Governors of the University of North Carolina, 704 F. 2d 713 (4th Cir., 1983).

Jones v. State Board of Education, 279 F. Supp. 190 (M.D. Tenn., 1968) aff'd 407 F. 2d 834 (6th Cir., 1969).

Keene v. Rodgers, 316 F. Supp. 217 (D. Me., 1970).

Kelly v. Iowa State Educational Association, 372 N.W. 2d 288 (Iowa App. 1985).

Kraft v. Alanson White Psychiatric Foundation, 498 A. 2d 1145 (D.C. App. 1985).

Lightsey v. King, 567 F. Supp. 645 (E.D. N.Y., 1983).

McDonald v. Board of Trustees of University of Illinois, 375 F. Supp. 95 (N.D. Ill., 1974) aff'd 503 F. 2d 105 (1974).

Marshall v. Maguire, 424 N.Y.S. 2d 89 (1980).

Mary M. v. Clark, 473 N.Y.S. 2d 843 (A.D. 3 Dept., 1984).

Melton v. Bow, 247 S.E. 2d 100 (Ga., 1978).

Meyer v. University of Washington, 719 P. 2d 98 (Wash., 1986).

Miranda v. Arizona, 384 U.S. 436 (1966).

Moore v. Student Affairs Committee of Troy State University, 284 F. Supp. 725 (D.C. Ala., 1968).

Morale v. Grigel, 422 F. Supp. 988 (D. N.H., 1976).

Morris v. Slappy, 461 U.S. 1 (1983).

Morrissey v. Brewer, 408 U.S. 471 (1972).

Napolitano v. Princeton University Trustees, 453 A. 2d 263 (N.J. Super. A.D., 1982).

Nash v. Auburn University, 621 F. Supp. 948 (M.D. Ala., 1985).

NLRB v. Donnelly Garment Company, 330 U.S. 219 (1947).

National Union of Marine Cooks and Stewards v. Arnold, 348 U.S. 37 (1954).

New Jersey v. T.L.O., 469 U.S. 325, 83 L. Ed. 2d 720 (1985).

North v. West Virginia Board of Regents, 332 S.E. 2d 141 (W. Va., 1985).

Nzuve v. Castleton State College, 335 A. 2d 321 (Vt., 1975).

Patterson v. Hunt, 682 S.W. 2d 508 (Tenn. App., 1984).

Petrey v. Flaugher, 505 F. Supp. 1087 (E.D. Ky., 1981).

Picozzi v. Sandalow, 623 F. Supp. 1571 (E.D. Mich., 1986).

Pointer v. Texas, 380 U.S. 400 (1965).

Reetz v. Michigan, 188 U.S. 505 (1903).

Regents of University of Michigan v. Ewing, 474 U.S. ____, 88 L.Ed. 2d 523 (1985).

Rivera Carbana v. Cruz, 588 F. Supp. 80 (D. Puerto Rico, 1984).

Roberts v. United States, 445 U.S. 552 (1980).

St. Amant v. Thompson, 390 U.S. 727 (1968).

Shaughnessy v. United States, 345 U.S. 206 (1953).

Slaughter v. Brigham Young University, 514 F. 2d 622 (10th Cir., 1975).

Smyth v. Lubbers, 398 F. Supp. 777 (W.D. Mich., 1975).

Sofair v. State University of New York, 377 N.E. 2d 730 (N.Y., 1978).

Sohmer v. Kinnard, 53 F. Supp. 50 (D. Md., 1982).

Speake v. Grantham, 317 F. Supp. 1253 (S.D. Miss., 1970), aff'd 440 F. 2d 1351 (5th Cir., 1971).

Tedeschi v. Wagner College, 427 N.Y.S. 2d 760 (N.Y., 1980).

Turof v. Kibbee, 527 F. Supp. 880 (E.D. N.Y., 1981).

United States v. Grayson, 438 U.S. 41 (1978).

University of Houston v. Sabeti, 676 S.W. 2d 685 (Tex. App., 1984).

Uzzell v. Friday, 592 F. Supp. 1502 (M.D. N.C., 1984).

Wasson v. Trowbridge, 382 F. 2d 807 (2d Cir., 1967).

Webster v. Byrd, 494 So. 2d 31 (Ala., 1986).

Winnick v. Manning, 460 F. 2d 545 (2d Cir., 1972).

Wood v. Strickland, 420 U.S. 308 (1975).

Woody v. Burns, 188 So. 2d 56 (Fla. App., 1966).

Wright v. Texas Southern University, 392 F. 2d 728 (5th Cir., 1968).

Yench v. Stockmar, 483 F. 2d 820 (10th Cir., 1973).

Zanders v. Louisiana State Board of Education, 281 F. Supp. 747 (W.D. La., 1968).

Zissu v. Bear, Stearns & Company, 805 F. 2d 75 (2nd Cir., 1986).

Bibliography

American Council on Education (1983). Amicus Brief in *Mary M.* v. *Clark* 473 *N. Y. S.* 2d 843 (A.D. 3 Dept., 1984).

Amsden, D. (1981). Fraud in Academe. Phi Kappa Phi Il., 57, 37-44.

Andrews, K. R. (1985). Letter from the Editor. *Harvard Business Review, 63* (5), 1-2.

Astin, A. W. (1984). Student Values. Knowing More About Where We Are Today. *AAHE Bulletin, 36*(9), 10-13.

Barnett, D. C., & Dalton, J. C. (1981). Why College Students Cheat? *Journal of College Student Personnel, 22* 545-551.

Berglass, S. cited in Goleman, D. (August 24, 1986). The Strange Agony of Success. *New York Times* p. 1 Sect. 3.

Bok, D. (1983). A Flawed System. *Harvard Magazine,* (May-June) 38-71.

Bok, S. (1978). *Lying.* New York: Vintage Books.

Boodish, H. M. (1962). The Teacher's Page: School vs. Life. *The Social Studies, 53,* 149-153.

Bowen, H.R. (1980). *Investment in Learning: The Individual and Social Value of American Higher Education.* San Francisco: Jossey-Bass, Inc.

Boyce, W.D., & Jensen, L. C. (1978). *Moral Reasoning: A Psychological— Philosophical Integration.* Lincoln: The University of Nebraska Press.

Brown, P. (December 6, 1983). Misguided Lawyers. *New York Times,* p. A31.

Burger, W. (February, 1984). Remarks at the mid-year meeting of the American Bar Association. 1-18.

Bushway, A. & Nash, W. R. (1977). School Cheating Behavior. *Review of Educational Research, 47,* 623-632.

Buss, W. & Novak, M. (January 1980). The Detection of Cheating on Standardized Tests: Statistical and Legal Analysis. *Journal of Law and Education, 9,* 1-64.

Carnegie Council on Policy Studies in Higher Education (1979). *Fair Practices in Higher Education: Rights and Responsibilities in a Period of Intensified Competition for Enrollment.* San Francisco: Jossey-Bass, Inc.

97

Casper, J. (1972). *American Criminal Justice: The Defendant's Perspective.* Englewood Cliffs: Prentice-Hall. Cited in Silberman, 1978, p. 298.

Chickering, A. W. (1969). *Education and Identity.* San Francisco: Jossey-Bass, Inc.

Coles, R. (April 20, 1986). Conscience of a Psychiatrist. *The Washington Post,* H5.

Connell, C. (1981). Term Paper Mills Continue to Grind. *Educational Record,* summer, 1981, 19-28.

Craver, C. (1983). The Problem Solving Function of Legal Counselors. University of Illinois College of Law *Chronicle,* (spring) 4-5.

Dalton, J. C.; Healy, M. A.; & Moore, J. E. (1985). Planning a Comprehensive Values Education Program. In J. Dalton (Ed.). *Promoting Values Development in College Students* (63-76). NASPA Monograph Series; vol. 4.

David, R. L. & Kovach, J. A. (1979). Attitudes Toward Unethical Behavior as a Function of Educational Commercialization. *College Student Journal, 13,* 338-344.

Davis, K. (1971). *Discretionary Justice.* Urbana: Illini Books.

Davis, K. (1972). *Administrative Law Text.* St. Paul: West.

Dershowitz, A. (1982). *The Best Defense.* New York: Random House.

Drake, C. A. (1941, May 16). Why Students Cheat? *Journal of Higher Education,* 418-420.

Eddy, E. (1977, winter). What Happened to Student Values? *Educational Record,* 7-16.

Edwards, G. (February 23, 1987). A Nation of Liars. *U.S. News and World Report,* p. 60.

Evett, J. B. (1980). Cozenage: A Challenge to Engineering Instruction. *Engineering Education, 70,* 434-436.

Fagan, Brian M. (1984). *Lead Us Not Into Temptation: A Report and Recommendations on Academic Dishonesty at UCSB.* Unpublished manuscript, University of California - Santa Barbara, Santa Barbara.

Fair Practices in Higher Education. (1979). Carnegie Council on Policy Studies in Higher Education. San Francisco: Jossey Bass, Inc.

Frankel, M (1975). The Search for Truth: An Umpireal View. *University of Pennsylvania Law Review, 123,* 1031-1059.

Freedman, S. (December 4, 1986). Outcry Raised in Levin Case at Blame-the-Victim Defense. *New York Times,* p. 1.

Freshman Characteristics and Attitudes. (1986, July 23). *The Chronicle of Higher Education,* 35-36.

Friendly, H. (1975). Some Kind of Hearing. *University of Pennsylvania Law School, 123,* 1267-1317.

Gehring, D.; Nuss, E. M.; and Pavela, G. (1986). Issues and Perspectives on Academic Integrity. Columbus, Oh.: NASPA, Inc.

Gilligan, C. (1982). *In a Different Voice: Psychological Theory and Women's Development.* Cambridge: Harvard University Press.

Grant G. (1981). The Character of Education and the Education of Character. *Daedalus*, (summer, 1981).

Hardy, R. J. (1982). Preventing Academic Dishonesty: Some Important Tips for Political Science Professors. *Teaching Political Science, 9*(2), 68-77.

Hardy, R. J. & Burch, D. (1981). What Political Science Professors Should Know in Dealing With Academic Dishonesty. *Teaching Political Science, 9* (1), 5-14.

Hereford, F. (November 30, 1984). Letter to Those Expressing Concern Over the Recent Honor Trial of Olden Polynice, 1-3.

Hersh, R. H., Paolitto, D. P., & Reimer, J. (1979). *Promoting Moral Growth from Piaget to Kohlberg.* New York: Longman, Inc.

Hesburgh, T. M. (1985). The Role of the Academy in a Nuclear Age. In J. B. Bennett & J. W. Peltason (Eds.). *Contemporary Issues in Higher Education.* New York: Macmillan Publishers.

Hesburgh, T. (1987). Cited in McLoughlin, M. A Nation of Liars? *U.S. News and World Report*, February 23, 1987, 54-60.

Houston, J. P. (1976a). Amount and Loci of Classroom Answer Copying, Space Seating, and Alternate Test Forms. *Journal of Educational Psychology, 68,* 729-735.

Houston, J. P. (1976b). The Assessment and Prevention of Answer Copying on Undergraduate Multiple-Choice Examinations. *Research in Higher Education, 5,* 301-311.

Huckaby, G. (1983). Cited in Peters, C. Tilting at Windmills. *Washington Monthly*, (October, 1983), 8.

Hughes, G. (June 24, 1982). Busting the People's Case. *New York Review of Books*, 27-29.

Kaplin, W. (1978). *The Law of Higher Education.* San Francisco: Jossey-Bass.

Kirp, D. L. (1976). Proceduralism and Bureaucracy: Due Process in the School Setting. *Stanford Law Review, 26,* 841-876.

Knefelkamp; L. L., Widick, C.; & Parker, C. (1978). *New Directions in Student Services: Applying New Developmental Findings.* San Francisco: Jossey-Bass, Inc.

Kohlberg, L. (1971). Stages of Moral Development as a Basis for Moral Education. In C.M. Beck, B. S. Crittendon, & E. V. Sullivan (Eds.), *Moral Education: Interdisciplinary Approaches*, 23-92. Toronto: University of Toronto Press.

Kohlberg, L. (1975). The Cognitive Developmental Approach to Moral Education. *Phi Delta Kappan, 56,* 670-677.

Kohlberg, L. (1976). Moral Stages and Moralization: The Cognitive Development Approach. In T. Lickona (Ed.) *Moral Development and Behavior*, 31-53. New York: Holt, Rinehart and Winston.

Kohlberg, L., & Kramer, R. (1969). Continuities and Discontinuities in Childhood and Adult Moral Development. *Human Development, 12,* 93-120.

Kouzes, J. (March 8, 1987). Why Businessmen Fail in Government. *New York Times*, F3.

Krebs, R. L. (1968). *Some Relationships between Moral Judgment, Attention, and Resistance to Temptation.* (Doctoral Dissertation, University of Chicago, 1967). American Doctoral Dissertations, 158.

LaBier, D. (1986). *Modern Madness.* Boston: Addison-Wesley.

Lamm, N. (October 14, 1986). A Moral Mission for Colleges. *New York Times*, A35.

Lamont, L. (1979). *Campus Shock.* New York: E. P. Dutton.

Leming, J. S. (1978). Cheating Behavior, Situational Influence, and Moral Development. *Journal of Educational Research, 71,* 214-217.

Levine, A. (1980). *When Dreams and Heroes Died: A Portrait of Today's College Students.* San Francisco: Jossey-Bass, Inc.

Long, N. (1985). Standard of Proof in Student Disciplinary Cases. *Journal of College and University Law, 12,* 71-81.

Martineau, R. (November, 1984). Frivolous Appeals: The Uncertain Federal Response. *Duke Law Journal, 1984,* 845-886.

Montor, K. (1971). Cheating in High School. *School and Society, 99,* 96-98.

Morrill, R. L. (1980). *Teaching Values in College.* San Francisco: Jossey-Bass, Inc.

Morris, H. (1981, October) A Paternalistic Theory of Punishment. *American Philosophical Quarterly,* 263-271.

Mueller, K. H. (1953). Can cheating be killed? *Personnel and Guidance Journal, 31,* 465-468.

Neff, M. & Nagel, S. (1974). The Adversary Nature of the American Legal System from a Historical Perspective. *New York Law Forum, 20,* 123-164.

Neely, R. (June, 1983). Loser Pays Nothing: Why Our Courts are Overcrowded. *Washington Monthly,* 40-48.

Newman, F. (1985). *Higher Education and the American Resurgence.* Princeton: The Carnegie Foundation for the Advancement of Teaching.

Novak, M. (1982). *The Spirit of Democratic Capitalism.* New York: Touchstone.

Nuss, E. M. (1981). Undergraduate Moral Development and Academic Dishonesty. (Doctoral dissertation, University of Maryland, 1981) *Dissertation Abstracts International, 42,* 3463A.

Nuss, E. M. (1984). Academic Integrity: Comparing Faculty and Student Attitudes. *Improving College and University Teaching, 32*(3), 140-144.

On My Honor . . . Philosophy and Guidelines of the Honor System. University of Virginia (undated), 1-23.

Parrott, Fred J. (1972). How to Cheat the Cheaters. *Improving College and University Teaching, 20,* 128-130.

Pavela, G. (1978). Judicial Review of Academic Decision Making after Horowitz. *School Law Journal, 55*(8), 55-75.

Pavela, G. (1981, February 9). Cheating on Campus. Who's Really to Blame? *The Chronicle of Higher Education,* 64.

Pavela, G. (1983) in Gehring, D. (Ed.) *Administering College and University Housing: A Legal Perspective.* Asheville, College Administration Publications.

Pavela, G. (1985). *The Dismissal of Students with Mental Disorders.* Asheville, College Administration Publications.

Pavela, G. (1986, Winter). Student Discipline and Psychotherapy: Different Voices and Harmonious Objectives. *Journal of College Student Psychotherapy,* 41-49.

Perry, W. (1981). Cognitive and Ethical Growth. In A. Chickering (Ed.). *The Modern American College.* San Francisco: Jossey-Bass, Inc.

Project on Redefining the Meaning and Purpose of Baccalaureate Degrees. (1985). *Integrity in the College Curriculum: A Report to the Academic Community.* Washington, D.C.: Association of American Colleges.

Prosser, W. (1964). *The Law of Torts.* St. Paul: West.

Rest, J. R. (1979). *Development in Judging Moral Issues.* Minneapolis: University of Minnesota Press.

Rest, J. R. (1983). Morality. In J. Flavell & E. Markman (Eds.), *Cognitive Development: Vol. IV.* In P. Mussen (General Ed.), *Manual of Child Psychology.* New York: Wiley.

Rest, J. R. (1985). Evaluating Moral Development. In J. Dalton (Ed.), *Promoting Values Development in College Students* (77-90). NASPA Monograph Series; vol. 4.

Richardson (1973). *Richardson on Evidence.* Brooklyn: Brooklyn Law School.

Rosenberg, N. & Birdzell, L. (1986). *How the West Grew Rich.* New York: Basic Books.

Sandeen, A. (1985). The Legacy of Values Education in College Student personnel Work. In J. Dalton (Ed.). *Promoting Values Development in College Students* (1-16). NASPA Monograph Series; vol. 4.

Sanford, N. (1962). *The American College.* New York: Wiley.

Sanford, N. (1966). *Self and Society.* New York: Atherton Press.

Sanford, N. & Axelrod, J. (1979). *College and Character.* Berkeley, Ca. Montaigne, Inc.

Shirk, E. & Hoffman, R. W. (1961). The Academic Setting of a Dishonest Student. *Improving College and University Teaching,* 9, 130-134.

Silberman, C. (1978). *Criminal Violence, Criminal Justice.* New York: Random House.

Singhal, A. C. & Johnson, P. (1983). How to Halt Student Dishonesty. *College Student Journal,* 17 (1), 13-19.

Smith, G. (1964). *When the Cheering Stopped—The Last Years of Woodrow Wilson.* New York: William Morrow & Company. Cited in *Clayton* v. *Trustees of Princeton University,* 608 F. Supp. 413, 415 (D. N.J., 1985).

Solomon, R. & Hanson, K. (1985). *Its Good Business.* New York: Atheneum.

Solzhenitsyn A. (1980). In Berman (Ed) *Solzhenitsyn at Harvard.* Washington, D.C.: Ethics and Public Policy Center.

St. Clair, R. E. (1976). A Study of the Changes in Moral Judgment Patterns of College Students. (Doctoral dissertation, University of Virginia, 1975). *Comprehensive Dissertation Index, 5*, DAH 76-0032.

Steele, B.; Johnson, D.; & Rickard, S. (1983). Managing the Judicial Function in Student Affairs. Unpublished paper, 1-26. A shorter version is published in *Journal of College Student Personnel* (July, 1984) 337-342.

Steininger, M.; Johnson, R. E.; & Kirts, D. K. (1964). Cheating on College Examinations as a Function of Situationally Aroused Anxiety and Hostility. *Journal of Educational Psychology, 55*, 317-324.

Stevens, G. (1975). The Reputation Rights of Students. *Journal of Law and Education, 4*, 623-631.

Stone, M. (1977, September 19). The Crime of Cheating. *U. S. News and World Report*, 92.

Strick, A. (1977). *Injustice for All*. New York: Putnam's Sons.

Students' Honesty Stays at High Level Over Two Decades. (1981, February). *The Sanford Observer*, 1, 4.

Study Group on the Conditions of Excellence in American Higher Education. (1984). *Involvement in Learning: Realizing the Potential of American Higher Education*. Washington, D.C.: National Institute of Education.

Tittle, C. R. & Rowe, A. R. (1974). Fear and the Student Cheater. *Change, 6*(3), 47-48.

Tribe, L. (1978). *American Constitutional Law*. Mineola: Foundation Press.

Twenty-three Students Allegedly Cheated in Psychology I Examination. (1985, October). *The Stanford Observer*, 1, 11.

Turiel, E. (1966). An Experimental Test of the Sequentiality of Developmental Stages in the Child's Moral Development. *Journal of Personality and Social Psychology, 3*, 611-618.

Uhlig, G. E. & Howes, B. (1967). Attitude Toward Cheating and Opportunistic Behavior. *Journal of Educational Research, 60*, 411-412.

Vitro, F. T. (1971). The Relationship of Classroom Dishonesty to Perceived Parental Discipline. *Journal of College Student Personnel, 12*, 427-429.

Webber, L. J.; McBee, J. K.; & Krebs, J. E. (1983). Take Home Tests: An Experimental Study. *Research in Higher Education, 18*, 473-483.

Wellborn, S. N. (1980, October 20). Cheating in College Becomes an Epidemic. *U. S. News and World Report*, 39, 42.

Welsh, P. (1986). *Tales Out of School*. New York: Viking. Cited in *The Harvard Education Newsletter*, March, 1987, 1-8.

Williams, F. M. (1969). Cheating in the Classroom. *Improving College and University Teaching, 17*, 183-184.

Wilson, J. & Herrnstein, R. (1985). *Crime and Human Nature*. New York: Simon and Schuster.

Resources for Legal Information in Secondary and Higher Education

If you have found the information contained in this monograph to be helpful in your day-to-day operations and as a reference it is quite likely that you may also be interested in other titles included in the *The Higher Education Administration Series* or in our publications that offer quarterly updates on case law related to various fields of education.

At the back of this book is a form for ordering other titles available from College Administration Publications. When you place your order you may wish to copy the form rather than tearing out the page.

Other titles in *The Higher Education Administration Series:*

► Administering College and University Housing:
   A Legal Perspective

► The Dismissal of Students with Mental Disorders:
   Legal Issues, Policy Considerations
   and Alternative Responses

► Computers in Education:
   Legal Liabilities and Ethical Issues
   Concerning Their Use and Misuse

► A Practical Guide to Legal Issues Affecting Teachers

► Faculty / Staff Nonrenewal and Dismissal for Cause
   in Institutions of Higher Education

► A Guide to Successful Searches for College Personnel:
   Policies, Procedures, and Legal Issues

The following publications offer the reader a quarterly report on recent precedent setting higher court decisions covering a wide range of subjects in the area encompassed by the self-descriptive title. In addition, through the accumulated back issues, and in the "College" publications, a casebook, each of these publications are also excellent comprehensive references that can be of great help in day-to-day operations and long range planning:

► The College Student and the Courts

► The College Administrator and the Courts

► The Schools and the Courts
   While primarily written for practicing administrators, superintendents, school boards, teachers and legal counsel in secondary education, this publication is of great value to related schools of education.

Order Blank

Bill to:........................... Ship to:.....................

....

....

Quantity	Item & Price	Total

MONOGRAPHS

_____ The Dismissal of Students with Mental Disorders: _____
　　　　1 to 9 copies @ $9.95; 10 or more copies @ $9.50

_____ Administering College and University Housing: _____
　　　　1 to 9 copies @ $9.95; 10 or more copies @ $9.50

_____ A Practical Guide to Legal Issues Affecting
　　　　College Teachers _____
　　　　1 to 9 copies @ $4.95; 10 to 24 copies @ $3.95;
　　　　　　　　　　　　25 or more copies @ $3.50

_____ Computers in Education: Legal Liabilities and
　　　　Ethical Issues Concerning Their Use and Misuse _____
　　　　1 to 9 copies @ $9.95; 10 or more copies @ $9.50

_____ Faculty / Staff Nonrenewal and Dismissal for Cause
　　　　in Institutions of Higher Education _____
　　　　1 to 9 copies @ $9.95; 10 or more copies @ $9.50

_____ A Guide to Successful Searches for College Personnel:
　　　　Policies, Procedures, and Legal Issues _____
　　　　1 to 9 copies @ $9.95; 10 or more copies @ $9.50

_____ Academic Integrity and Student Development:
　　　　Legal Issues and Policy Perspectives _____
　　　　1 to 9 copies @ $9.95; 10 or more copies @ $9.50

PERIODICALS

_____ The College Student and the Courts
　　　　Includes casebook, all back issues and four
　　　　quarterly updating supplements............$98.50 _____

_____ The College Admir᾽ rator and the Courts
　　　　Includes caseᵇ , all back issues and four
　　　　quarterly uр g supplements............$99.50 _____

_____ The Sc Courts
　　　　Incluᴄ) pages of back issues and four
　　　　updating ᴛs........................$67.50 _____

　　　　　　　　Postage (if payment accompanies
　　　　　　　　order we will ship postpaid) _____

　　　　North Carolina residents add appropriate sales tax _____

　　　　　　　　　　　　　　　　　Total _____

Address Orders to:
College Administration Publications, Inc.
Dept. SS, P.O. Box 8492, Asheville, NC 28814

☐ Pricing of the above publications was correct on the publication date of this monograph. If you wish to be advised of current prices of titles you have ordered before shipment, please check.

☐ For further information regarding any of the above titles please indicate with check here and in the quantity column of each publication and we will forward current brochures and information.